THE MERMAID COOKBOOK

THE MERMAID COOKBOOK

Mermaid's Purse Mirror Glaze Cake (pp.29–31) and Wave Cake (pp.35–37) recipes by Amy Hunter; Oyster Biscuits (pp.52–53) and Mermaid Cheesecake (pp.113–115) recipes by Claire Berrisford

An Hachette UK Company
www.hachette.co.uk

Summersdale Publishers Ltd
Part of Octopus Publishing Group Limited
Carmelite House
50 Victoria Embankment
LONDON
EC4Y 0DZ
UK

www.summersdale.com

Printed and bound in Malta

ISBN: 978-1-78685-731-6

Substantial discounts on bulk quantities of Summersdale books are available to corporations, professional associations and other organisations. For details contact general enquiries: telephone: +44 (0) 1243 771107 or email: enquiries@summersdale.com.

THE MERMAID COOKBOOK

ALIX CAREY

summersdale

For Harley and Harper

ABOUT THE AUTHOR

Alix Carey is a baking enthusiast from Surrey who combined her passions for creativity and writing when she launched her blog My Kitchen Drawer in 2015. My Kitchen Drawer is a baking biography showcasing Alix's journey through colourful, fun recipes, baking advice, reviews and general kitchen-life musings. Alix is a self-confessed dreamer and is the author of *The Unicorn Cookbook*.

Follow her on Instagram and Twitter **@mykitchendrawer**.

🐚 CONTENTS 🐚

Introduction **8**
What Is Your Mermaid Name? **9**
Conversions and Measurements **10**
Kitchen Essentials **11**

🐚 CUPCAKES 🐚
Heart of the Ocean Cupcakes **16**
Mermaid Scale Cupcakes **18**
Octopus Cupcakes **20**
Dive into the Ocean Cupcakes **22**
Coral Reef Buttercream **25**

🐚 CELEBRATION CAKES 🐚
Mermaid's Purse Mirror Glaze Cake **29**
Mermaid Kisses Cake **32**
Wave Cake **35**
Ultimate Diving Mermaid Cake **38**
Sandcastle Showstopper **41**

🐚 COOKIES AND BISCUITS 🐚
Jam Clams **46**
Sea Holly Shortbread **48**
Rock Pool Cookies **51**
Oyster Biscuits **52**
Hermit Crab Cookies **55**

🐚 BARS AND BITES 🐚
Pebble Pretzel Bites **58**
Mermaid Kisses **60**
Mermaid Energy Balls **63**
Stormy Sea Brownies **64**
Mermazing Fudge **67**
Fish Doughnuts **68**

Seaweed Coconut Bars **71**
Magical Mermaid Rocks **73**

 **PARTY FOOD**
Pearl of the Ocean Macarons **76**
Coral Reef Eclairs **78**
Shark Teeth Kebabs **81**
Mermaid Marshmallow Crispy Bars **83**
Pearl Cake Pops **85**
Octopus Arm Churros **88**
Seabed Rocky Road **91**
Personalised Mermaid Tail Biscuits **93**
Mesmerising Madeleines **97**
Jellyfish Layered Surprise **99**

 BREAKFAST
Mermaid Toast **103**
Starfish Pancakes **104**
Tropical Sea Smoothie Bowl **107**
Turtle Waffles **109**

 DESSERTS
Mermaid Cheesecake **113**
Seafoam Mousse **117**
Under the Sea Ice Lollies **119**
Tropical Swiss Roll **120**
Coral Fruit Tarts **123**

DRINKS
Mertastic Milkshake **127**
Sea Breeze Slushie **129**
Lemonade Float **131**
Sealicious Chia Seed Smoothie **133**

My Recipe Notes **135**
Index **142**

INTRODUCTION

Welcome to *The Mermaid Cookbook*, where all your under-the-sea wishes are guaranteed to come true in the form of delicious treats. Inside this magical book you'll find 46 fun-filled recipes, ready to help you bring the mysterious mermaids out of the water and into the kitchen. But before you begin Operation Mermaid, you need to find your oceanic name. So, what are you waiting for? On the next page, you'll be able to identify your fantasy alter-ego and begin your baking adventure into the world of the most mesmerising aquatic legend of all time.

WHAT IS YOUR MERMAID NAME?

To discover your mermaid name, find the initial of your first name and the month you were born in the lists below. Combine the two and state your new alias aloud with joy as you don your apron and get ready to dive into this magical mermaid feast.

A - MOONSHINE
B - PEBBLE
C - PEARL
D - AQUATA
E - JEWEL
F - PACIFICA
G - CORAL
H - TREASURE
I - SHIMMERING
J - GLISTENING
K - SASSY
L - SPARKLING
M - GLOSSY
N - LUNA
O - STORMY
P - MELODY
Q - COVE
R - FIERCE
S - BRAVE
T - RADIANT
U - CRYSTAL
V - ROYAL
W - BUBBLE
X - MARINE
Y - BAY
Z - SEA QUEEN

JANUARY - SHORE DREAMER
FEBRUARY - MAGIC SCALES
MARCH - TWILIGHT STAR
APRIL - SEA GLIDER
MAY - EMERALD WATERS
JUNE - AQUA ANGEL
JULY - WHISPER WAVE
AUGUST - GOLDEN GODDESS
SEPTEMBER - SUNSHINE REEF
OCTOBER - TIDE DANCER
NOVEMBER - MOONLIGHT GEM
DECEMBER - GLITTER TAIL

CONVERSIONS AND MEASUREMENTS

All the conversions in the tables below are close approximates, which have been rounded up or down. When using a recipe always stick to one unit of measurement and do not alternate between them.

LIQUID MEASUREMENTS
6ml = 1 tsp
15ml = 1 tbsp
30ml = ⅛ cup
60ml = ¼ cup
120ml = ½ cup
240ml = 1 cup
2 tbsp liquid egg white = 1 large egg white

BUTTER MEASUREMENTS
30g = ⅛ cup
55g = ¼ cup
75g = ⅓ cup
115g = ½ cup
150g = ⅔ cup
170g = ¾ cup
225g = 1 cup

DRIED INGREDIENT MEASUREMENTS
5g = 1 tsp
15g = 1 tbsp
150g flour = 1 cup
225g caster sugar = 1 cup
115g icing sugar = 1 cup
175g brown sugar = 1 cup
200g sprinkles = 1 cup

OVEN TEMPERATURES

°C	°F	Gas mark
140	275	1
150	300	2
170	325	3
180	350	4
190	375	5
200	400	6
220	425	7
230	450	8
240	475	9

KITCHEN ESSENTIALS

Before we get started, let's take a look at all the essential ingredients and equipment you'll need.

INGREDIENTS

Butter – Unsalted butter is best for baking and it is easiest to use at room temperature, but when you're making pastry it needs to be cold.

Flour – Most of these recipes call for regular plain flour, but occasionally, when baking cakes, I advise using self-raising flour.

Sugar – The most important types of sugar for the recipes in this book are caster sugar, icing sugar and light muscovado sugar.

Flavour extracts – A number of recipes in this book require vanilla extract, but there are several others that call for other flavours, such as peppermint, if you wish to use these.

Eggs – Always use large eggs, unless otherwise specified.

Gel food colouring – These are preferred over liquid food colourings because, most importantly, they do not dilute any mixtures and, secondly, you only need to add a few drops to make rich, vibrant colours.

Sprinkles and edible glitter – You'll have a hard task getting through this book without sprinkles and edible glitter. The key cake decorations you will need are: nonpareils (tiny balls made of sugar and starch), edible star sprinkles, dragées (edible pearls), sugar crystals and edible glitter.

Edible candy eyes – A few recipes also use edible eyes to help bring your bakes to life. Edible candy eyes can be found in the cake-decorating section of most supermarkets, in cake-decoration shops or online.

White chocolate – Whether it be for dipping, coating, drizzling or even baking, white chocolate is a big part of many of these recipes. Of course, you are welcome to use dark or milk chocolate as a replacement, but white chocolate is used widely as its appearance can be changed easily with food colouring.

Desiccated coconut – To add that tropical touch to many recipes in this book, it's worth making sure your cupboard is well-stocked with this ingredient.

Lemon and lime zest – To help add some fresh flavours to your delicious sweet treats.

Cream cheese – This is used in a number of recipes in the book. Don't worry if you're dairy-free as you can simply replace dairy cream cheese with soya or other non-dairy options.

EQUIPMENT

Baking trays/tins – You will need at least three flat sheet baking trays, a 27cm x 20cm tray bake tin, a Swiss roll tin and a 20cm square brownie tin.

Cake/cupcake tray – All the cakes in this book are baked in round 18cm or 20cm cake tins and you will need at least two of each (maximum of six). All cupcakes are baked in batches of 12 so you will need a 12-hole cupcake tray as well as a 12-hole mini cupcake tray.

Sugar thermometer – When making confectionery items, mirror glaze and Italian meringue buttercream, a sugar thermometer will make the recipes failsafe and easier to follow.

Baking paper – The majority of recipes will ask you to line a baking tray or cake tin so baking paper is a necessity. (*Note: this is not to be confused with greaseproof paper, which is not heat resistant and can cause baked goods to stick to it like glue. Baking paper has a silicon lining and is heat resistant, which prevents any cakes or baked goods from sticking to it.*)

Mixing bowls – An assortment of sizes would be ideal, but as long as you have one heatproof mixing bowl you'll get through this book just fine.

Piping bags – Piping bags are used throughout this book for piping buttercream, meringues and batter. You could make your own out of sandwich bags but you'll never achieve the perfectly piped cupcake that way. Piping bags, especially those with a grip, allow you to pipe with absolute accuracy and precision so I would always recommend having a large stash in your kitchen drawer.

Piping nozzles – These come in all shapes and sizes to create a variety of decorations, but I most commonly use the star tips (closed and open), which create decorative swirls and wave patterns, and large round tips for macarons, meringue kisses, cake covering and creating those all-important mermaid scales.

Palette knife – The palette knife is a great tool for creating the mermaid scale effect and covering your large cakes with icing.

Cookie cutters – You will find these in a huge variety of shapes and sizes, but it's the star shapes you'll need for this book. You can purchase packets of these cutters in every size possible from most high-street kitchen retailers.

Fondant/chocolate moulds – Mermaid tail and seashell moulds are used several times throughout this book. You could make the recipes without them but they do add the perfect finishing touch to any mermaid recipe so I would recommend using them.

Rolling pin – A kitchen necessity for bashing biscuits (for a cheesecake base) as well as rolling out pastry.

Cupcake cases – When making cupcakes, you'll need cupcake cases and you can be as adventurous as you wish with the colours. Blues, greens, turquoise, purples and pinks, as well as metallic colours, are the perfect choice for these recipes.

Electric whisk or standing mixer – While I advocate the use of your own mermaid strength, you'll find an electric whisk or standing mixer much easier and quicker for many of these recipes.

Scales – Baking is a science and requires precise measurements of ingredients.

Measuring spoons – My baking besties. A little lesson to remember: a teaspoon is 5ml and a tablespoon is 15ml. Avoid using normal cutlery to approximate these, as they can range between 2ml and 10ml. This might not sound like much difference, but a sponge cake can crack or sink on as little as a few grams too much or too little baking powder.

Icing smoother – The perfect tool for creating that perfectly smooth buttercream on all your celebration cakes.

Decorating turntable – A 360-degree rotating table makes icing cakes a doddle and allows for easy piping, smoothing and decorating.

CUPCAKES

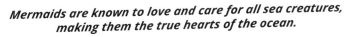

HEART OF THE OCEAN CUPCAKES

Mermaids are known to love and care for all sea creatures,
making them the true hearts of the ocean.

Makes: 12 ◦ **Time: 2 hours** ◦ **Difficulty rating:** ★ ★

INGREDIENTS

For the hearts:

* 200g butter, softened
* 200g caster sugar
* 3 eggs
* 200g self-raising flour
* ¼ tsp raspberry flavouring
* Pink gel food colouring

For the cupcakes:

* 150g butter, softened
* 150g caster sugar
* 3 eggs
* 150g self-raising flour
* ¼ tsp vanilla extract

For the buttercream:

* 200g butter, softened
* 400g icing sugar
* Purple gel food colouring

EXTRA EQUIPMENT

You will need a 12-hole cupcake tray, two 20cm cake tins, 12 cupcake cases, a 2cm heart-shaped cookie cutter, a piping bag and a closed-star piping nozzle.

METHOD

For the hearts:

Preheat the oven to 180°C and line two 20cm cake tins with baking paper.

Add the butter, sugar, eggs and flour to a large mixing bowl and beat together until pale and fluffy. Add the raspberry flavouring and a drop of pink gel food colouring, then mix through until well combined.

Pour the mixture equally between the two cake tins and bake for 20–25 minutes. Leave to cool.

Once cooled, cut out six hearts from each cake tin using the cookie cutter and put to one side.

For the cupcakes:

Keep the oven at 180°C and line a cupcake tray with 12 cupcake cases.

Add the butter, sugar, eggs and flour to a large mixing bowl, and beat together until pale and fluffy. Add the vanilla extract and mix through until well combined.

Fill each cupcake case with a tablespoon of batter, then carefully place a sponge heart into the centre of each cupcake, pushing it down until it is almost completely submerged in the batter. Bake in the oven for 20–25 minutes until just browned and springy to touch, then leave to cool on a wire rack.

For the buttercream:

Blend the butter and icing sugar together until smooth, add a few drops of the purple gel food colouring (enough to make the buttercream a pastel colour) and combine.

Fit a piping bag with a closed-star nozzle, transfer the mixture into the piping bag and pipe swirls of buttercream on top of the cupcakes.

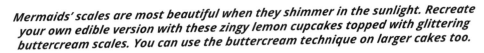

MERMAID SCALE CUPCAKES

Mermaids' scales are most beautiful when they shimmer in the sunlight. Recreate your own edible version with these zingy lemon cupcakes topped with glittering buttercream scales. You can use the buttercream technique on larger cakes too.

Makes: 12 ❀ **Time: 2 hours** ❀ **Difficulty rating:** ★ ★

INGREDIENTS

For the cupcakes:

- ★ 150g butter, softened
- ★ 150g light brown sugar
- ★ 3 eggs
- ★ 150g self-raising flour
- ★ Zest of 1 lemon

For the buttercream:

- ★ 200g butter, softened
- ★ 400g icing sugar
- ★ Zest of 1 lemon
- ★ Gel food colouring of your choice
- ★ Edible silver glitter

EXTRA EQUIPMENT

You will need a 12-hole cupcake tray, 12 cupcake cases, a piping bag, a round-hole piping nozzle and a small palette knife.

METHOD

For the cupcakes:

Preheat the oven to 180°C and line a cupcake tray with 12 cupcake cases.

Add the butter, sugar, eggs and flour to a large mixing bowl, and beat together until pale and fluffy. Add the lemon zest and mix through until well combined.

Fill each cupcake case with a tablespoon of batter and bake in the oven for 20–25 minutes until just browned and springy to touch.

Remove from the oven and leave to cool on a wire rack.

For the buttercream:

Blend the butter and icing sugar together until smooth, add the lemon zest and a good few drops of gel food colouring (enough to make the buttercream a vibrant colour), and combine.

Fit a piping bag with a round-hole nozzle, transfer the buttercream mixture into the piping bag and pipe one row of dots along the top of the cupcake.

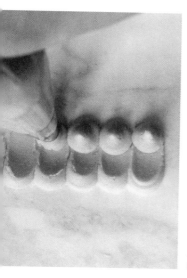 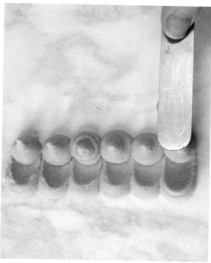 

Using the back of a teaspoon or a small palette knife, spread the buttercream dots out to create the appearance of a scale. Repeat both steps on the next row and the row after until you have completely covered the cupcake.

Finish with a sprinkle of silver edible glitter and serve.

🐚 OCTOPUS CUPCAKES 🐚

Octopuses spread so much love to their underwater friends that they need three hearts to contain it. These squishy, cute octopus cupcakes are guaranteed to make your heart melt.

Makes: 12 🐚 Time: 2 hours 🐚 Difficulty rating: ⭐ ⭐

INGREDIENTS

For the cupcakes:

* 150g butter, softened
* 150g light brown sugar
* 3 eggs
* 150g self-raising flour
* 50g desiccated coconut

For the buttercream:

* 200g butter, softened
* 400g icing sugar
* 1 tsp vanilla extract
* Turquoise gel food colouring

For the octopuses:

* 200g white chocolate
* Orange gel food colouring
* 12 white marshmallows
* 24 edible candy eyes

EXTRA EQUIPMENT

You will need a 12-hole cupcake tray, 12 cupcake cases, a baking tray, baking paper, a closed-star piping nozzle, a writing-tip piping nozzle and two piping bags.

METHOD

For the cupcakes:

Preheat the oven to 180°C and line a cupcake tray with 12 cupcake cases.

Add the butter, sugar, eggs and flour to a large mixing bowl, and beat together until pale and fluffy. Add the desiccated coconut and mix through until well combined.

Fill each cupcake case with a tablespoon of batter and bake in the oven for 20–25 minutes until just browned and springy to touch.

Remove from the oven and leave to cool on a wire rack.

For the buttercream:

Blend the butter and icing sugar together until smooth, add the vanilla extract and a drop of turquoise gel food colouring (enough to make the buttercream a pale-green tone), and combine.

Fit a piping bag with a closed-star nozzle, transfer the buttercream mixture into the piping bag and pipe swirls on top of each cupcake.

For the octopuses:

Prepare a baking tray with baking paper and set aside.

Place the white chocolate in a heatproof bowl over a pan of simmering water. Leave the chocolate to melt completely, stirring occasionally, then add ¼ teaspoon orange gel food colouring and stir it through. Take the bowl off the heat and leave the chocolate to cool slightly.

When the chocolate is cool enough to hold your finger in without burning it, you can begin dipping your marshmallows. Pierce the end of a marshmallow with a fork or a cocktail stick and dip it into the orange-coloured chocolate, coating it fully. Remove the marshmallow from the fork and let it sit on the baking tray to set a little. Continue the previous steps with the remaining marshmallows.

Stick the candy eyes to the chocolate-coated marshmallows while the chocolate is still sticky, then carefully place them on top of the buttercream once the chocolate has completely set.

Tip the remaining orange chocolate into a piping bag fitted with a writing-tip nozzle and pipe the octopus arms either side of the marshmallow and down the sides of the buttercream.

Leave to set completely then serve.

❀ DIVE INTO THE OCEAN CUPCAKES ❀

Create a splash with these simple-to-make but beautifully
detailed lime-flavoured mermaid cupcakes.

Makes: 12   ❀   **Time: 2 hours**   ❀   **Difficulty rating:** ⭐⭐

INGREDIENTS

For the cupcakes:

* 150g butter, softened
* 150g light brown sugar
* 3 eggs
* 150g self-raising flour
* Zest of 1 lime

For the buttercream:

* 200g butter, softened
* 400g icing sugar
* Zest of 1 lime
* Turquoise and purple gel food colouring
* Edible silver glitter

For the decorations:

* 200g white chocolate
* 50g brown sugar
* Edible pearl sprinkles

EXTRA EQUIPMENT

You will need a 12-hole cupcake tray, 12 cupcake cases, two medium-sized piping bags, a large piping bag, a closed-star piping nozzle, a small mermaid tail mould and seashell moulds.

METHOD

For the cupcakes:

Preheat the oven to 180°C and line a cupcake tray with 12 cupcake cases.

Add the butter, sugar, eggs and flour to a large mixing bowl, and beat together until pale and fluffy. Add the lime zest and mix through until well combined.

Fill each cupcake case with a tablespoon of batter and bake in the oven for 20–25 minutes until just browned and springy to touch.

Remove from the oven and leave to cool on a wire rack.

For the buttercream:

Blend the butter and icing sugar together until smooth, add lime zest and combine.

Split the mixture equally between two bowls, adding 1–2 drops purple gel food colouring to one bowl and 1–2 drops turquoise gel food colouring to the other, mixing each until your icing reaches a pastel tone.

Fill two piping bags with the buttercream, one for each colour, then cut the ends and place both into a larger piping bag fitted with a closed-star nozzle.

Pipe swirls of the buttercream on to each cupcake.

For the decorations:

Break the white chocolate into small pieces, place them in a heatproof bowl over a pan of simmering water and, stirring occasionally, let the chocolate melt down completely.

Split the melted chocolate equally into three bowls and colour one turquoise, one purple – using 1–2 drops of food colouring for each – and leave the other plain.

Fill the mermaid and seashell moulds with a little amount from each of the bowls of chocolate, then mix it around a little with a cocktail stick. Put the moulds in the freezer to set hard for 5 minutes.

Repeat until you have enough decorations for all 12 cupcakes, then carefully place the mermaid tails on top of each of the cupcakes and place one or two chocolate shells next to it. Finish with a dusting of brown sugar and a few pearl sprinkles and serve.

🐚 CORAL REEF BUTTERCREAM 🐚

In the summer months, mermaids migrate to Italy for the warm weather but also to taste the silky Italian meringue buttercream for which the country is renowned.

Makes: Enough to ice 12 cupcakes 🐚 **Time: 45 minutes** 🐚
Difficulty rating: ★ ★ ★

INGREDIENTS

* 100ml water
* 300g caster sugar
* 5 large egg whites
* 500g butter, softened
* Pinch of salt
* 1 tsp vanilla extract
* Gel food colouring (pink, purple, yellow and green)

EXTRA EQUIPMENT

You will need a sugar thermometer, an electric whisk, four piping bags, a closed-star piping nozzle, an open-star nozzle, a grass-tip nozzle and a small petal-tip nozzle.

METHOD

This is quite a complicated set of instructions where timing and forward planning are everything, but once you've made one batch of buttercream you'll realise that it's actually quite straightforward.

Before you begin making the buttercream, bake 12 cupcakes using the exact ingredients and method for the Mermaid Scale Cupcakes on page 18.

Firstly, pour 100ml water into a saucepan and add 250g of the caster sugar. On a medium heat, stir the ingredients until the sugar dissolves to create a syrup. Then place your thermometer in the pan and bring the mixture to the boil without stirring it. Now turn your attention to the egg whites.

Prepare a large bowl of cold water and set it to one side near the hob for later.

In another large bowl, begin whisking the egg whites with an electric whisk until they hold stiff peaks. Gradually whisk in the remaining caster sugar and continue for 5 minutes until the mixture can be held upside down without it falling out of the bowl. Now you have meringue.

Returning to your syrup, check the temperature and as soon as it reaches 121°C, remove the pan from the heat and plunge the base of it into the bowl of cold water for 3 seconds. This stops the mixture from getting any hotter.

Next, gradually pour the syrup in a thin stream into your meringue mix, gently whisking on low speed all the while. Be careful when pouring, as if the liquid strays too close to the edge of the bowl, it will set there, and if it's poured over the moving whisk, the hot syrup may spit everywhere. Continue whisking the mixture for about 8–10 minutes until the bowl feels just lukewarm.

The next stage is to gradually whisk in the butter followed by the salt and vanilla extract. The mixture may look like it has curdled at first but, as you continue to whisk it, it will form a smooth buttercream.

Split the mixture equally between four bowls and add ¼ teaspoon of the gel food colouring to each bowl so you have four pastel shades of buttercream. Using four piping bags, fit each one with the different piping nozzles. Add the pink buttercream to the closed-star nozzle bag, the purple buttercream to the open-star nozzle bag, the green buttercream to the petal-tip nozzle bag and the yellow buttercream to the grass-tip nozzle bag.

Start by piping the pink swirls on each cupcake, followed by the purple then fill the gaps with the yellow and the green.

CELEBRATION CAKES

❧ MERMAID'S PURSE MIRROR ❧ GLAZE CAKE

The mermaids' purses you find washed up on the beach are actually the egg cases of sharks and rays. This mermaid's purse cake is a shimmering reflection of their deep purple hue and, what's more, it's edible!

Serves: 12–16 ❧ Time: 2 hours plus overnight freezing for the cake; 1 hour 30 minutes for the Mermaid Kisses ❧ Difficulty rating: ★ ★ ★

INGREDIENTS

For the cake:

* 200g self-raising flour
* 200g butter, softened
* 200g caster sugar
* 3 eggs
* ½ tsp baking power
* ½ tsp vanilla extract

For the buttercream:

* 200g butter, softened
* 400g icing sugar

For the glaze:

* 12g gelatine powder
* 135ml water (60ml for the gelatine)
* 150g granulated sugar
* 140g liquid glucose

* 100g sweetened condensed milk
* 150g white chocolate chips
* Purple gel food colouring

For the decorations:

* Dark chocolate chips
* Mermaid Kisses (see page 60). These take approx. 1 hour and 30 minutes to make. They can be stored in an airtight container for 7–10 days if you wish to make them ahead of baking the cake.
* Handful blackberries and blueberries

EXTRA EQUIPMENT

You will need two 20cm cake tins, a 20cm diameter cake board, a palette knife, an immersion blender, a sugar thermometer and a cocktail stick.

METHOD

For the cake:

Preheat the oven to 180°C and line two 20cm cake tins with baking paper.

Mix the flour, butter, sugar, eggs, baking powder and vanilla in a bowl and beat together until smooth, pale and fluffy, then fill the two cake tins with the batter, making sure they're level, and bake for 20 minutes.

Remove from the oven and leave to cool in the tins for 15 minutes before lifting out and placing on a wire rack to cool completely.

For the buttercream:

Combine the butter and icing sugar and mix until smooth, pale and fluffy.

Assembling the cake:

Assemble the cake by adding a little white buttercream to a 20cm cake board and placing one of the sponges on top. Add 2 tablespoons of buttercream to the top of the sponge, spread it out across the entire surface and then add the second sponge on top of the first.

Cover the entire cake with a thick layer of buttercream and smooth it out with a palette knife. The smoother your buttercream looks at this stage, the better finish you will get with the mirror glaze. (*Note: mirror glaze works better on a frozen cake so ideally you want to freeze the cake overnight before adding the glaze.*)

For the glaze:

Stir the gelatine into lukewarm water in a small bowl and leave to one side for later.

In a saucepan, boil the sugar, water and glucose until it reaches 103°C. Take the pan off the heat and whisk in the gelatine. Then whisk the condensed milk into the mixture.

Add the contents of the pan to a heatproof bowl with the white chocolate chips and your gel food colouring – enough to make the chocolate a vibrant purple – and gently stir the mixture very briefly. Then blend for about 1–2 minutes. You don't want to add air to the mixture so try not to move the blender too much.

Leave the mixture to cool to around 30–32°C, gently stirring occasionally to prevent a skin from forming and popping any air bubbles on the surface with a cocktail stick.

It is best to check the consistency of your glaze before pouring it on to the cake by using the back of a spoon. If the glaze covers and sticks to the back of the spoon, with a small amount of run-off, then it is the perfect pouring temperature. If your glaze is too cold and stiff, put it in the microwave or on the stove for a few seconds.

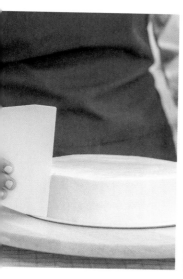  

When you are ready to use the glaze, take your frozen cake from the freezer and put it on top of a wire rack so that the excess glaze can drain through. Pouring mirror glaze is very messy so a good tip is to put a tray underneath the wire rack to catch the excess.

Pour the mirror glaze over the cake, ensuring the top and sides are completely covered. Any excess on the top can be wiped away using a palette knife.

Leave the glaze to dry before decorating.

For the decorations:

Scatter the dark chocolate chips around the base of the cake and place Mermaid Kisses on top of the cake along with a handful of blueberries and blackberries.

🐚 MERMAID KISSES CAKE 🐚

Baking this cake requires a big heart and a caring soul. The difficulty is finding the elusive mermaids to help top it off with their kisses!

Serves: 10–12 🐚 **Time: 2–3 hours** 🐚 **Difficulty rating:** ★ ★

INGREDIENTS

For the cake:

* 300g self-raising flour
* 300g butter, softened
* 300g caster sugar
* 6 eggs
* 1 tsp baking powder
* 1 tsp vanilla extract

For the buttercream:

* 500g butter, softened
* 1kg icing sugar
* 1 tsp vanilla extract
* Turquoise gel food colouring

For the decorations:

* Mermaid Kisses (see page 60) – these take approx. 1 hour and 30 minutes to make. They can be stored in an airtight container for 7–10 days if you wish to make them ahead of baking the cake.

EXTRA EQUIPMENT

You will need two 18cm cake tins, a 20cm diameter cake board, a palette knife, an icing smoother and a decorating turntable.

METHOD

For the cake:

Preheat the oven to 180°C and line two 18cm cake tins with baking paper.

Place the flour, butter, sugar, eggs, baking powder and vanilla extract into a bowl and whisk together for 2–3 minutes until smooth, pale and fluffy.

Divide the cake batter between the two lined cake tins and bake for 25–30 minutes.

Remove from the oven and leave to cool in the tins for 15 minutes before lifting out and placing on a wire rack to cool completely. Once cool, cut the two sponge cakes in half so you have four layers ready for assembling.

For the buttercream:

Put the butter in a bowl and beat until smooth, then add the icing sugar and vanilla extract and continue mixing until smooth and pale.

Add a drop of turquoise gel food colouring, enough to create a mint-green tone, and mix thoroughly.

To assemble:

Add a little buttercream to the 20cm cake board so that your first sponge layer can be secured to the base. Continue sandwiching the remaining sponge layers, with a generous portion of the mint-green buttercream in between each layer.

Cover the entire cake with a thin layer of the mint-green buttercream and smooth it out with a palette knife, then leave in the fridge for an hour to harden.

Add a second, thicker coat of the mint-green buttercream, then use a palette knife to smooth it around. Place the cake on the decorating turntable, take your icing smoother, holding it lightly on the cake with the bottom touching the turntable, and rotate the cake. If you need to go around the cake again, clean your icing smoother and repeat.

Cover the cake in Mermaid Kisses.

🐚 WAVE CAKE 🐚

If you like making waves in the kitchen, this recipe is for you. Surprise your guests when you cut into the cake and reveal its different shades of the ocean.

Serves: 20 🐚 Time: 2–3 hours 🐚 Difficulty rating: ★ ★

INGREDIENTS

For the cake:

- ★ 500g self-raising flour
- ★ 500g butter, softened
- ★ 500g caster sugar
- ★ 6 eggs
- ★ 1 tsp baking power
- ★ 1 tsp vanilla extract
- ★ Blue gel food colouring

For the buttercream:

- ★ 400g butter, softened
- ★ 800g icing sugar
- ★ Blue gel food colouring
- ★ White gel food colouring (optional)

EXTRA EQUIPMENT

You will need three 20cm cake tins, a 25cm diameter cake board, a palette knife, an icing smoother and a decorating turntable.

METHOD

For the sponge:

Preheat the oven to 180°C and line the 20cm cake tins with baking paper. This cake will need to be baked in batches unless you have a very big oven.

Add the flour, butter, sugar, eggs, baking powder and vanilla extract to a bowl, and mix together until smooth, pale and fluffy. You may want to add half the ingredients to one bowl and the other half to another to make it easier to mix.

Split the batter equally between six bowls and add blue gel food colouring to five of them, ensuring they are different shades of blue, ranging from pale to dark. Add the food colouring in very small amounts so you are able to achieve a good range of blues.

Fill three cake tins with three of the six batters, making sure they are level, then place the tins into the pre-heated oven and bake for 20 minutes or until you can insert a skewer into the sponge and it comes out clean.

Remove from the oven and leave to cool in the tins for 15 minutes before lifting out and placing on a wire rack to cool completely.

Repeat the above with the remaining three bowls of batter.

For the buttercream:

Combine the butter and icing sugar and mix until smooth, pale and fluffy. Separate a third of the mixture into a bowl and colour with blue gel food colouring until nice and vibrant. The rest of the buttercream might look a little yellow so you may wish to add a little white gel food colouring to the remaining buttercream, but this is optional.

Assembling the cake:

Layer the cake together by adding a little white buttercream to a 25cm cake board and sticking the darkest blue layer on top. Add a tablespoon of buttercream to the top of the sponge layer and spread it out across the entire surface, then add the next darkest blue sponge. Repeat and continue with the other blue sponges, getting lighter for each layer. Leave the plain sponge to one side for decoration later.

Cover the entire cake with a thin layer of buttercream and smooth it out with a palette knife. Leave in the fridge for an hour until the buttercream has hardened.

To create the ombre effect:

Sit your cake on a decorating turntable and, starting at the bottom, spread the blue icing using your palette knife so that it completely covers the sponge. Once you reach the middle of the cake, spread the white icing and the blue icing alternately, cleaning your palette knife in between. Don't worry about being neat at this stage or if the colours start mixing together. As you move towards the top of the cake spread the white icing around the cake. You do not need to use lots of icing for this, but enough so that when you smooth it out, there will be no cake showing through.

Once all the colours have been blended together with a palette knife, it's time to smooth them together using an icing smoother. For best results, place the icing smoother edge lightly on the cake, with the bottom touching the turntable, and rotate the cake around, continuing until the surface is smooth. If you need to go around the cake again, clean your icing smoother and repeat. If you can see the sponge through the icing, add more icing to the area and repeat with the icing smoother.

For the top:

Randomly add white and blue buttercream blobs on to the top of the cake with your palette knife so that the entire surface is covered. Using your palette knife, swirl patterns in the buttercream on top so that the two colours mix together and create a wave effect.

For the decoration:

Either using your hands or a blender, crush the plain sponge layer that you put to one side into crumbs so that it resembles sand. Using the remaining buttercream, stick the crushed sponge to the cake board next to the bottom of the cake.

❧ ULTIMATE DIVING MERMAID CAKE ❧

One taste of this gorgeous lemon showstopper and you'll be diving in for more.

Serves: 10–12 ❧ Time: 2–3 hours ❧ Difficulty rating: ★ ★

INGREDIENTS

For the cake:

* ★ 400g self-raising flour
* ★ 400g butter, softened
* ★ 400g caster sugar
* ★ 6 eggs
* ★ 1 tsp baking powder
* ★ Zest of 1 lemon

For the Italian meringue buttercream:

* ★ 100ml water
* ★ 300g caster sugar
* ★ 5 large egg whites
* ★ 500g butter, softened
* ★ Pinch of salt
* ★ Zest of 1 lemon
* ★ Gel food colouring (orange, purple and turquoise)

For the decorations:

* ★ 50g white chocolate
* ★ Silver edible glitter

EXTRA EQUIPMENT

You will need two 18cm cake tins, a 20cm diameter cake board, a palette knife, an icing smoother, a decorating table, three piping bags, two open-star nozzles, a closed-star nozzle and a mermaid tail mould.

METHOD

For the cake:

Preheat the oven to 180°C and line two 18cm cake tins with baking paper.

Place the flour, butter, sugar, eggs, baking powder and lemon zest into a bowl and whisk together for 2–3 minutes until smooth, pale and fluffy.

Divide the cake batter between the two lined cake tins and bake for 20–25 minutes.

Remove from the oven and leave to cool in the tins for 15 minutes before lifting out and placing on a wire rack to cool completely. When cool, cut the two sponge cakes in half so you have four layers ready for assembling.

For the Italian meringue buttercream:

Follow steps 3–8 for Coral Reef Italian Meringue Buttercream on pages 25–26 to make the Italian meringue buttercream, replacing the vanilla extract with lemon zest. Then split the mixture equally between two bowls, colouring one half a light mint green with a drop of turquoise gel food colouring. Split the other half between two bowls and add a drop of the purple gel food colouring to one bowl and a drop of the orange gel food colouring to the other bowl, and mix until well combined.

Assembling and decorating the cake:

Melt the white chocolate in a bowl set over a pan of simmering water, or in a microwave, and fill a mermaid tail mould. Leave in the fridge to set. Repeat until you have two mermaid tails ready for decoration.

Add a little buttercream to the 20cm cake board so that your first sponge layer can be secured to the base. Continue sandwiching the remaining sponge layers with a generous portion of the mint-green buttercream in between each layer.

Cover the entire cake with a thin layer of the green buttercream and smooth it out with a palette knife, then leave in the fridge for an hour to harden.

Add a second, thicker coat of the mint-green buttercream (leaving a few tablespoons to one side for piping later), then use a palette knife to smooth it around. Take your icing smoother and place it lightly on the cake, with the bottom touching the turntable, and rotate the cake. If you need to go around the cake again, clean your icing smoother and repeat.

Add the three different coloured buttercreams to three separate piping bags, using the closed-star nozzle for the green buttercream, and the open-star nozzles for the orange and purple buttercream.

Pipe different coloured swirls on to the top and down one of the sides of the cake, add the two white chocolate mermaid tails on top and a dusting of silver glitter, then serve.

🐚 SANDCASTLE SHOWSTOPPER 🐚

A trip to the seaside is not complete without building a sandcastle and now, with the help of a little mermaid magic, you can create your own edible version. This recipe has many layers and stages, but masterpieces are worth the time and effort and, more importantly, it tastes incredible.

Serves: 25–30 🐚 **Time: 3 hours** 🐚 **Difficulty rating:** ★ ★ ★

INGREDIENTS

For the cake:

* 600g self-raising flour
* 600g butter, softened
* 600g caster sugar
* 12 eggs
* 2 tsp baking powder
* 400g fresh raspberries, crushed
* 2 tsp vanilla extract

For the buttercream:

* 1kg butter, softened
* 2kg icing sugar
* 2 tsp vanilla extract

For the filling:

* 200g raspberry jam

For the edible sand:

* 200g digestive biscuits
* 100g soft brown sugar

For the decorations:

* Two ice-cream cones
* 100g pink fondant
* 100g orange fondant
* 100g white chocolate (optional)

EXTRA EQUIPMENT

You will need two 20cm cake tins, two 15cm cake tins, a 15cm diameter cake board, a 24cm diameter cake board, a palette knife, an icing smoother, a piping bag, a cake-decorating piping nozzle, a decorating turntable, four dowel rods, a serrated knife, a cake lifter, a food processor, two thick paper straws, a small round-tip piping nozzle and seashell moulds.

METHOD

(Note: the windmill decorations should ideally be made ahead of time as they need to dry out overnight before they are secured on to the cake.)

For the cake:

Preheat the oven to 180°C and line two 20cm cake tins and two 15cm cake tins with baking paper.

Place the flour, butter, sugar, eggs and baking powder into a large bowl and whisk together for 2–3 minutes until smooth, pale and fluffy.

In a separate bowl, crush the raspberries with a fork, leaving some partially whole, then tip them into the cake batter with the vanilla extract and gently fold them in.

Divide the cake batter between all four lined cake tins and bake the 20cm cakes for 30–35 minutes and the 15cm cakes for 20 minutes.

Remove from the oven and leave in the tins for 15 minutes before lifting the cakes out and placing them on a wire rack to cool completely. Once cool, cut the four sponge cakes in half, horizontally, so you have eight layers ready for assembling.

For the buttercream:

Put the butter in a bowl and beat until smooth, then gradually add the icing sugar and vanilla extract and mix together until smooth and pale.

Assembling the cake:

Add a little buttercream to the 15cm cake board and place one 15cm sponge layer on to it (keep aside the layer with the smoothest surface and use last). Add a tablespoon of raspberry jam and continue sandwiching the remaining 15cm sponge layers with jam.

Fit a piping bag with the cake-decorating piping nozzle and fill the bag with the buttercream. Cover the entire 15cm cake with a thin layer of buttercream and smooth it out with a palette knife, then leave in the fridge for an hour to harden.

Follow the same steps for the 20cm cake, but use the 24cm cake board and double the quantity of jam for each layer.

Add a second, thicker coat of the buttercream to both cakes then use a palette knife to smooth it around as best as you can. Place one of the cakes on the decorating turntable, take your icing smoother, holding it lightly on the cake with the bottom touching the turntable, and rotate the cake. If you need to go around the cake again, clean your icing smoother and repeat. Then repeat this with the other cake.

To stack the cakes, insert the four dowel rods close to the centre of the 20cm cake, so the 15cm cake covers them.

To cut your dowel rods to size, use a pencil to mark the height of the cake on one of them and then lift it out and cut it at the pencil mark with a serrated knife. (*Note: it's important that the top of the dowel rod sits flush with the top of the cake so that the cake you layer on top has something to sit on.*) Discard or put the rest of the dowel rod to one side, so you know which one you should use.

Remove the rest of the dowels from the cake and, using the first dowel as a guide, cut them to equal size. Sand the tips down to smooth them out and avoid splintering, then insert all four dowels back into the cake. Using a cake lifter, carefully stack the 15cm tier on top. Don't worry if you get a few finger marks in the buttercream as you can smooth this back out when the cake is stacked and in position.

For the edible sand:

Put the biscuits and sugar into a food processor and blitz until the biscuits are very fine crumbs.

While the buttercream is still wet, take handfuls of the edible sand (making sure you leave some of the biscuit mixture for the decorations) and gently press it on to the two tiers of the cake until they are fully covered.

For the decorations:

Coat two ice-cream cones with buttercream, position them on the back of the top tier of the cake and cover with the remaining edible sand mixture.

For the polka-dot windmill, roll out the orange fondant to 0.5cm thickness and cut out a 10cm x 10cm square.

Roll out the pink fondant to 0.5cm thickness and, using the round-tip piping nozzle, cut out around ten small circles. Press the pink circles into the orange-fondant square in a random formation.

Repeat the process with the remaining fondant but reverse the colours (orange dots on pink fondant) or you could create a stripy windmill by using a rolling pin to press strips of one of the fondants into the other 10cm x 10cm fondant. (*Note: always make sure that the 'finished' fondant is a perfect square – otherwise creating the windmill shape won't work.*)

Using your knife, make four diagonal slits, starting at each corner of the fondant and finishing approximately 1.5cm from the centre of the fondant.

Wet the centre of the fondant slightly with a little water and place the tip of one of the straws on top of it. This will be your windmill handle.

Pick up one corner of the fondant and bend it inwards so that the tip reaches the centre. Press it down so it sticks to the fondant centre and covers a section of the straw.

Repeat with the three other corners until you have the windmill shape, then roll a small ball of fondant and stick it to the centre to cover where all the corners meet.

Repeat these steps with the other fondant square and straw.

Let the fondant dry out overnight then, when ready, insert one windmill to the bottom tier and another to the top tier.

As a final touch, decorate with white chocolate shells made by melting down 100g of white chocolate in a bowl set over a pan of simmering water. Fill the seashell moulds with the white chocolate and leave in the fridge to set hard for 20 minutes. When ready, carefully remove the chocolates from the moulds and decorate at the base of each tier for a realistic sandcastle effect.

COOKIES AND BISCUITS

🐚 JAM CLAMS 🐚

Take a bite of these buttery clams and discover a hidden pearl upon a bed of delicious strawberry jam.

Makes: 10 🐚 Time: 45 minutes 🐚 Difficulty rating: ⭐

INGREDIENTS

For the biscuits:

* ★ 250g unsalted butter, softened
* ★ 50g icing sugar
* ★ 2 tsp vanilla extract
* ★ 250g plain flour
* ★ 50g cornflour
* ★ 2–3 tbsp milk

For the filling:

* ★ 50g strawberry jam
* ★ 50g white fondant icing

EXTRA EQUIPMENT

You will need a piping bag and an open-star piping nozzle.

METHOD

For the biscuits:

Preheat the oven to 180°C and line two baking trays with baking paper.

Put the butter and icing sugar in a large bowl and beat with a whisk until pale and fluffy. Add the vanilla extract and beat again until well incorporated.

Sift in the flour and cornflour, then fold them into the butter mixture using a spatula until combined. Add the milk and mix it through (the dough should feel sticky).

Spoon the dough into a piping bag fitted with a large open-star piping nozzle.

Pipe swirls at about 5cm diameter on to two baking trays, leaving 3cm between each swirl.

Bake for 10–12 minutes until a pale-golden colour and cooked through. Leave to cool on the baking trays for a few minutes before transferring to cool fully on a wire rack.

For the filling:

While the biscuits are cooling, make your fondant pearls by rolling out a 5g piece of fondant into a smooth ball. You want to make ten pearls in total.

When the biscuits are cool, pair them up and turn one half upside down so the flat side is facing up. Spoon a teaspoon of jam on to the flat side and lay a fondant pearl towards the front. Top with the other biscuit, resting it on top of the jam and pearl at an angle to make it look like it is slightly open.

Repeat with the remaining biscuits and serve.

🐚 SEA HOLLY SHORTBREAD 🐚

If you can't find any sea holly growing along the coast or on the dunes when you next visit the seaside, try making these biscuit versions in your kitchen instead. Very delicious and definitely not spiky.

Makes: 12–14 🐚 Time: 2 hours 30 minutes 🐚 Difficulty rating: ⭐

INGREDIENTS

For the shortbread:

* 100g salted butter
* 40g caster sugar
* 150g plain flour
* 25g cornflour

For the icing:

* 400g royal icing
* 3–4 tbsp water
* Blue gel food colouring

EXTRA EQUIPMENT

You will need a 6cm star cutter, two piping bags and a writing-tip piping nozzle.

METHOD

For the shortbread:

Preheat the oven to 180°C and line a large baking tray with baking paper.

In a bowl, combine the butter and sugar together until soft and fluffy, then add the flour and cornflour and stir until the mixture forms a firm dough.

Place the dough on a lightly floured surface and knead gently until smooth, then roll out to a thickness of half a centimetre.

Using a 6cm star cutter, cut out 14 rounds and arrange them on the baking tray, spaced slightly apart, then chill in the fridge for 30 minutes.

Bake for 10–15 minutes until lightly golden, then allow to cool for 5 minutes before transferring to a wire rack to cool completely.

For the icing:

Put the royal icing into a large mixing bowl and stir in enough water until it reaches the consistency of toothpaste. Split the mixture between two bowls and add a drop of the blue gel food colouring to one bowl to create a light blue colour.

Leave the bowl filled with white icing to one side.

Split the light blue icing mixture in half again and in one of the bowls add a few more drops of water to loosen the consistency a little.

Fit one piping bag with a writing-tip nozzle and fill it with the thick blue icing. Carefully pipe around the star shape to create an outline and then leave to one side to allow the icing to set for 15 minutes.

Once set, fill a second piping bag with the looser light blue icing and slowly fill the centre of the stars with the icing. Put the icing to one side and allow it to set for 1 hour.

Lastly, fit a final piping bag with a writing-tip nozzle and, using the white icing, pipe on the details (you can copy the photo or be as creative as you like) and set aside to harden for another hour before serving.

❀ ROCK POOL COOKIES ❀

A rock pool is a special place filled with hidden treasures. Replicate your own foodie version and uncover the tasty treasure hiding in between two delicious cookies.

Makes: 15 ❀ **Time: 45 minutes** ❀ **Difficulty rating:** ★

INGREDIENTS

* ★ 125g butter
* ★ 150g dark chocolate (minimum 70 per cent cocoa)
* ★ 225g caster sugar
* ★ 3 eggs
* ★ 1 tsp vanilla extract
* ★ 250g plain flour
* ★ 150g cocoa powder
* ★ ½ tsp baking powder
* ★ Tub of ice cream, your choice of colour

METHOD

Preheat the oven to 180°C and line two baking trays with baking paper.

Melt the butter and chocolate in a heatproof bowl set over a pan of simmering water, then whisk the sugar, eggs and vanilla together in a separate bowl.

Leave the chocolate to cool a little, then fold the sugar and egg mixture into the chocolate.

Add the flour, cocoa powder and baking powder to the chocolate mixture and fold in gently.

Spoon the mixture on to the baking trays to make 30 biscuits (one tablespoon of mixture per biscuit should suffice), leaving a large enough gap between each, and bake in the oven for 6–8 minutes.

Remove from the oven and set aside half of the biscuits on a wire cooling rack. Turn the remaining biscuits over and place a small scoop of your desired ice cream on top of each.

Place the first set of cooled biscuits on top of the ice cream and eat immediately.

🐚 OYSTER BISCUITS 🐚

Recreate these magical underwater treasures in your very own kitchen.

Makes: 12 🐚 Time: 1 hour 30 minutes 🐚 Difficulty rating: ★ ★

INGREDIENTS

For the biscuits:

- ★ 200g unsalted butter, softened
- ★ 70g icing sugar
- ★ 2 tsp vanilla extract
- ★ 180g plain flour
- ★ 20g cornflour
- ★ ½ tsp baking powder
- ★ ½ tsp salt
- ★ 2 tbsp milk (if needed)

For the icing:

- ★ 150g butter, softened
- ★ 300g icing sugar
- ★ 1 tsp vanilla extract
- ★ 1 tbsp milk (if needed)
- ★ Blue gel food colouring (optional)

For the pearls:

- ★ 30g white fondant icing

EXTRA EQUIPMENT

You will need an electric whisk, two piping bags and a large open-star piping nozzle.

METHOD

For the biscuits:

Preheat the oven to 180°C and line two large baking trays with baking paper.

Beat the butter and sugar together in a large bowl with an electric whisk. When the mixture is pale in colour, add the vanilla extract and beat again.

Sieve the flour, cornflour, baking powder and salt into the bowl and fold it into the mixture to combine. If the dough is very stiff at this stage, add a splash of milk, half a teaspoon at a time, until it is smoother. The dough should be smooth, slightly sticky to the touch, and it should hold its shape.

Fit a piping bag with a large open-star nozzle and fill it with the biscuit dough.

Pipe the biscuit rounds on to your baking paper in a swirl shape (pipe from the centre outwards). Keep the rounds roughly 3cm apart.

Bake the biscuits for 10–12 minutes, or until they are golden around the edges. When done, allow them to cool on the tray before transferring them to a cooling rack.

For the icing:

Put the butter and sugar in a large bowl and beat until pale and fluffy.

Add the vanilla extract and beat again.

At this stage, the mixture should be soft enough to run a spoon through, but strong enough to hold its shape. If the mixture is too stiff, add milk a drop at a time to loosen it.

Add a drop of blue gel food colouring and mix until it is well incorporated. Keep adding more colour by degrees until you reach the shade you want.

Cover the bowl with cling film and put to one side until you're ready to assemble the biscuits.

For the pearls:

Take a small piece of fondant icing and use your hands to roll it into a ball about 1cm wide. Repeat this as many times as you need to give you one pearl per oyster biscuit.

Assembling the biscuits:

Prepare a piping bag with a star-shaped nozzle and fill it with the buttercream icing.

Take one oyster biscuit and pipe a swirl of icing on to the flat side.

Place a pearl at the front of the swirl.

Take a second oyster biscuit and place it on top of the swirl, flat side towards the icing. It should be positioned at an angle to look like an open oyster.

🐚 HERMIT CRAB COOKIES 🐚

These are possibly the cutest crabs you'll ever have the pleasure to meet. Make sure you give them some edible sand (AKA brown sugar) to stand on when serving to create the ultimate beach scene.

Makes: 15 🐚 Time: 2 hours 🐚 Difficulty rating: ⭐

INGREDIENTS

For the ginger biscuits:

* ★ 200g plain flour
* ★ ½ tsp salt
* ★ 1 tsp baking powder
* ★ 1½ tsp bicarbonate of soda
* ★ 2 tsp ground ginger
* ★ 100g unsalted butter
* ★ 100g caster sugar
* ★ 4 tbsp golden syrup
* ★ 1 tbsp milk

For the decorations:

* ★ 100g cream cheese
* ★ Red gel food colouring
* ★ 15 strawberries
* ★ 30 edible eyes
* ★ Soft brown sugar

EXTRA EQUIPMENT

You will need a 6cm circle cutter, a piping bag and a round-tip piping nozzle.

METHOD

For the ginger biscuits:

Preheat the oven to 180°C and line two baking trays with baking paper.

Combine the flour, salt, baking powder, bicarbonate of soda and ground ginger in a large bowl, then add the butter and rub the mixture together with your fingers to form what resembles breadcrumbs. Stir in the sugar.

In a separate bowl, mix the golden syrup and milk until the golden syrup dissolves. Stir this liquid into the breadcrumb mixture, then bring it all together with your hands to form a dough.

Break off small bits of dough and roll them into small balls roughly 20g in weight. Space 6–8 balls out on to each baking tray, ensuring you leave enough room for them to spread during baking.

Bake for 10 minutes until golden brown, but keep your eyes on them towards the end of baking as they can darken very quickly.

Once out of the oven, leave them on the trays for a few minutes to firm up, then transfer to a wire rack to fully cool.

For the decorations:

In a small bowl, combine the cream cheese with a small drop of red gel food colouring.

Fit a piping bag with a round-tip piping nozzle, transfer the cream cheese into the bag and pipe rounds on to each biscuit.

Cut off the tops of the strawberries to remove the stalks and use the remains of the tops to cut out small slices for the crab claws.

Assemble the crabs by placing the strawberries on top of the cream cheese rounds and placing two eyes underneath.

Stick the strawberry claws to the cream cheese, one either side of the eyes.

For added effect, sprinkle some soft brown sugar on top of the strawberries so it looks like the crabs have just dug themselves out of the sand.

BARS
AND
BITES

🐚 PEBBLE PRETZEL BITES 🐚

Who would have thought pebbles could be so yummy and soft?

Makes: 60   🐚   Time: 2 hours   🐚   Difficulty rating: ★ ★

INGREDIENTS

For the pretzels:

* ★ 64g light brown sugar
* ★ 470ml warm water (40°C)
* ★ 5½ tsp active dry yeast
* ★ 60ml vegetable oil
* ★ 750g plain flour
* ★ 100g bicarbonate of soda
* ★ 2 litres water
* ★ 1 egg, beaten

For the cinnamon sugar coating:

* ★ 100g caster sugar
* ★ 2 tbsp ground cinnamon
* ★ 35g butter

EXTRA EQUIPMENT

You will need three large baking trays.

METHOD

For the pretzels:

Grease a large bowl with oil and set aside.

In another large bowl, add the brown sugar and warm water, and stir until the sugar dissolves.

Sprinkle the yeast over the water and let it stand for about 5 minutes until foamy.

Stir in the vegetable oil and 450g of the flour until combined, then turn the dough out on to a floured surface and knead in the remaining 300g flour. The dough will be slightly sticky but continue kneading for around 3 minutes until smooth and silky. If the dough is very sticky add in a tablespoon of flour at a time until it's smooth.

Transfer the dough to the large greased bowl and cover it with cling film, then let it stand somewhere warm for about 1 hour until it has doubled in size.

Meanwhile, preheat the oven to 250°C and line three large baking trays with baking paper. Leave to one side for later.

When the dough has doubled in size, punch it down to release all the air and turn it out on to a floured surface. Knead the dough lightly then cut it into six equal rectangles.

Roll each section into rope-like shapes around 40cm long, then cut each section into about ten 1.5cm pieces. Leave to sit uncovered on the lined baking trays for 10 minutes.

To cook your pretzels, place 2 litres of water in a large saucepan with 100g of bicarbonate of soda and bring to a simmer over a high heat.

Reduce the heat to medium and, using two forks, carefully transfer six pretzel bites at a time to the simmering water and leave them for 30 seconds. Transfer each bite to a paper towel to drain, then return to the baking trays, spacing them evenly apart.

Continue this with the remaining bites.

Create an egg wash by cracking the egg into a bowl and whisking it together with a tablespoon of water, then brush each pretzel bite with the egg wash.

Bake in the oven for about 10 minutes until dark brown.

For the cinnamon sugar coating:

Combine the caster sugar and cinnamon together in a bowl and leave to one side.

Melt the butter gently in a pan and dip each baked pretzel bite into the butter and then into the cinnamon sugar mixture until fully coated.

Serve warm or at room temperature.

🐚 MERMAID KISSES 🐚

One kiss from a mermaid gives you gills and the ability to breathe underwater. If you haven't had the good fortune of receiving a kiss from a mermaid, these vibrant peaks of meringue are almost as exciting.

Makes: 24–30 🐚 Time: 1 hour 30 minutes 🐚 Difficulty rating: ★ ★ ★

INGREDIENTS

- ★ 75g caster sugar
- ★ 75g icing sugar
- ★ 3 egg whites
- ★ Turquoise and purple gel food colouring

EXTRA EQUIPMENT

You will need a piping bag, a round-tip piping nozzle and a clean cake-decorating paintbrush.

METHOD

Preheat the oven to 120°C and line two large baking trays with baking paper.

In a small bowl, mix both of the sugars together and set aside.

In a clean bowl, whisk the egg whites on a medium speed for 2 minutes until they form stiff peaks.

Begin adding the sugar a tablespoon at a time, whisking for 30 seconds between each tablespoon. Continue until you have used all the sugar and have a glossy meringue that holds stiff peaks.

Turn a piping bag inside out and using a paintbrush paint two lines of the turquoise gel food colouring followed by two lines of purple gel food colouring from the top to almost the end of the bag. Turn the piping bag back the right way so the painted lines are on the inside and fit it with a round-tip piping nozzle.

Fill with a few tablespoons of the meringue mix and twist the end to close. Holding the bag at a 90-degree angle over one of the lined trays, apply pressure at the start, then quickly draw the bag upwards to create little points. The painted-on colour will give the meringues the stripy pattern as they pass through the bag.

Pipe out around 12–15 meringue kisses on each baking tray and then bake in the oven for 1 hour or until they sound hollow when tapped.

Leave to cool in the oven, then store in an airtight container until ready to use.

These will keep in an airtight container for up to 7–10 days.

🐚 MERMAID ENERGY BALLS 🐚

These energy balls are perfect healthy snacks for times when you need to recharge your energy levels and give yourself a little mermaid strength.

Makes: 12 🐚 Time: 1 hour 30 minutes 🐚 Difficulty rating: ★

INGREDIENTS

* ★ 190g apricots
* ★ 100g dates, soaked
* ★ 50g desiccated coconut
* ★ 50g shredded coconut
* ★ 50g flaked almonds
* ★ 2 tbsp honey
* ★ 1 tsp vanilla extract

EXTRA EQUIPMENT

You will need a food processor.

METHOD

Line a baking tray with baking paper and set aside.

Put all the ingredients into a food processor and blitz for 1 minute until the mixture comes together.

Take a teaspoon of the mixture and roll it between your palms to form a ball. Leave it on the baking tray and repeat until you have used all the mixture.

Eat immediately or leave in the fridge for 20 minutes.

Keep refrigerated in an airtight container for 7 days or freeze in a freezer bag or container for up to three months.

🐚 STORMY SEA BROWNIES 🐚

It is often said that mermaids surface during storms to calm the seas and save those in danger. Bake up a storm with these brownies and watch all your fellow mermaids gather round to save you from eating the whole batch.

Makes: 16 🐚 Time: 1 hour 🐚 Difficulty rating: ★ ★

INGREDIENTS

For the brownie batter:

* 112g dark chocolate (minimum 70 per cent cocoa)
* 112g milk chocolate
* 150g unsalted butter
* 3 eggs
* 225g caster sugar
* 100g plain flour

For the cheesecake mixture:

* 250g cream cheese
* 50g caster sugar
* 1 egg yolk
* ¼ tsp peppermint extract
* Turquoise gel food colouring

EXTRA EQUIPMENT

You will need a 20cm square baking tin.

METHOD

For the brownie batter:

Preheat the oven to 170°C, and grease and line a 20cm square baking tin.

Melt the chocolate and butter in a heatproof bowl set over a pan of simmering water. Once the ingredients have melted, remove the bowl from the pan and set aside to cool slightly.

While the mixture cools, whisk the eggs and caster sugar in a large bowl until well combined. Add the eggs and sugar to the melted chocolate and butter, and whisk together for 1 minute.

Add the flour and carefully fold it into the mixture using a metal spoon until fully incorporated.

For the cheesecake mixture:

Beat the cream cheese, caster sugar, egg yolk and peppermint extract together until smooth.

Add a tiny drop of the turquoise gel food colouring and mix it in to create a mint colour.

Pour the brownie batter into the brownie tin, smoothing it out into all corners then spoon the mint cheesecake mixture

in a random formation on top. Using the tip of a knife, swirl the two mixtures together to give a marbled effect.

Bake in the oven for 25–30 minutes. Remove from the oven, leave in the tin and set aside to cool completely before peeling off the baking paper and cutting into equal squares.

🐚 MERMAZING FUDGE 🐚

Be mesmerised by the swirls and the taste of this indulgent white chocolate fudge.

Makes: 30 🐚 Time: 1 hour 15 minutes 🐚 Difficulty rating: ★

INGREDIENTS

* 400g good-quality white chocolate
* 397g can condensed milk
* 25g butter
* 100g icing sugar
* Turquoise gel food colouring
* Edible pearl sprinkles

EXTRA EQUIPMENT

You will need a 20cm square tin and baking paper.

METHOD

Line a 20cm square tin with baking paper and set to one side.

Break the chocolate into a non-stick saucepan, then add the condensed milk and butter. Melt the ingredients gently over a low heat, stirring occasionally until smooth.

Sieve in the icing sugar and mix thoroughly to remove any lumps, then pour the mixture into the lined tin and smooth over.

Add a few drops of turquoise gel food colouring and swirl it around the fudge mixture to create a marbled effect.

Decorate with pearl sprinkles and chill in the fridge for 1 hour until set.

To serve, cut it into squares and store in an airtight container in the fridge for up to two weeks.

🐚 FISH DOUGHNUTS 🐚

Transform plain old ring doughnuts into a school of multi-coloured fish with this recipe.

Makes: 8 🐚 Time: 2 hours 🐚 Difficulty rating: ★ ★ ★

INGREDIENTS

For the doughnuts:

- ★ 300g strong white flour, plus extra for dusting when kneading
- ★ 25g caster sugar
- ★ 75g unsalted butter, softened
- ★ 2 eggs
- ★ 2 tsp instant yeast
- ★ 1 tsp salt
- ★ 75ml warm milk
- ★ 1 litre sunflower oil, for frying

For the decorations:

- ★ 200g icing sugar
- ★ Different coloured sugar-coated chocolate drops
- ★ 8 edible eyes

EXTRA EQUIPMENT

You will need an 8cm circle cutter and a 2cm circle cutter.

METHOD

For the doughnuts:

Place all the ingredients, except the sunflower oil, into a large bowl then add 3 tablespoons of water and stir with your hands to make a dough. Gradually add another tablespoon of water and knead it in.

Tip the dough on to a lightly floured surface and knead well for 10 minutes, or until the dough becomes smooth and elastic.

Place the dough in a bowl, cover with a damp tea towel and leave to rise somewhere warm for 40 minutes.

When it has doubled in size, tip the dough out again on to a very lightly floured surface and divide it in half.

With a floured rolling pin, roll out the dough to about 1cm thick and cut out eight circles using the 8cm circle cutter. Using the 2cm cutter, cut smaller circles out of the middle of each 8cm circle.

Spin each doughnut on your index finger to expand the hole a little.

Place the doughnuts on to an oiled baking tray, loosely cover with cling film and leave to rise for 30 minutes.

Frying the doughnuts:

(*Safety note: cooking with hot oil can be dangerous and safety instructions should be followed to avoid accidents. Before frying, ensure young children are kept away from the pan and you are*

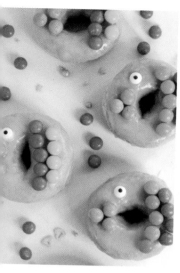
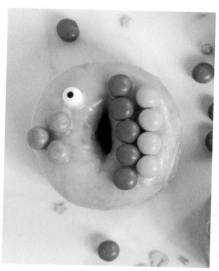
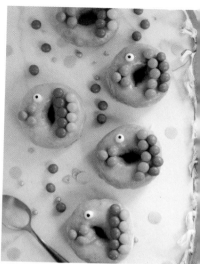

protected by wearing long sleeves. Never leave a pan of oil heating on a stove unattended. Use a large sturdy pan and keep the pan's handles away from the front of the cooker to avoid knocking it off the hob. While frying, keep your eyes away from the pan in case the oil spits at you. Have a large slotted spoon ready to lift out the doughnuts.)

Prepare two baking trays with baking paper and place them near to where you will be frying your doughnuts. Fill a large deep pan with sunflower oil and heat to 180°C.

Carefully drop the doughnuts in one at a time, cooking each side for about a minute or until golden-brown. Remove with a slotted spoon, place on to the lined baking tray and leave to cool.

For the decorations:

Put the icing sugar into a large bowl and gradually add 25ml of cold water to it, mixing it to create a thick paste.

When the doughnuts have cooled, dip the tops of them into the icing. Leave to set slightly for 5 minutes.

When the icing is still a little sticky, create the scales by placing five of the same coloured chocolates on one half of the doughnut, surrounding the ring. Then add four different coloured chocolates next to the first row. To create the face, add an edible eye and three chocolates that are a different colour to the ones on the other side of the doughnut in a triangle shape.

Leave to set on a cooling rack before serving and eat within 24 hours.

❧ SEAWEED COCONUT BARS ❧

One bite of these coconut bars and you will take your taste buds on an underwater adventure.

Makes: 12 ❧ Time: 2 hours ❧ Difficulty rating: ★

INGREDIENTS

* 200g desiccated coconut
* 397g condensed milk
* Pinch of salt
* Blue gel food colouring
* 100g dark chocolate (minimum 70 per cent cocoa)
* 200g milk chocolate
* Silver and turquoise edible glitter

EXTRA EQUIPMENT

You will need a 30cm x 15cm baking tin, baking paper and a large mixing bowl.

METHOD

Line a baking tin with baking paper and set aside.

In a large bowl, mix the desiccated coconut, condensed milk, salt and blue gel food colouring until well combined.

Fill the baking tin with the mixture and smooth it out, packing it down as you go. Put in the freezer to set hard for around 1 hour.

Once set, cut it into equal 10cm x 3cm rectangles and pop back into the freezer while you melt the chocolate.

Set a heatproof bowl over a pan of simmering water and melt the dark and milk chocolate together. Leave the chocolate to cool slightly, then remove the coconut bars from the freezer and dip each one into the chocolate using two forks. Place the coated bars back on the lined baking tray and sprinkle over the edible glitter.

Leave on a baking tray and let the chocolate set for 30 minutes before transferring to the fridge or somewhere cold for an hour. These will keep for 3 days if stored somewhere cool in an airtight container.

MAGICAL MERMAID ROCKS

Adorned with edible pearls and a shimmer of glitter,
these Magical Mermaid Rocks will be a hit at any party.

Makes: 1 slab   Time: 1 hour 15 minutes   Difficulty rating: ★

INGREDIENTS

* 400g white chocolate
* Pink and turquoise gel food colouring
* Edible pearl sprinkles
* Edible silver glitter

EXTRA EQUIPMENT

You will need one baking tray, baking paper, a cocktail stick and a mermaid tail mould (optional).

METHOD

Line a baking tray with baking paper and set aside.

Place the squares of white chocolate in a heatproof bowl over a pan of simmering water and, stirring occasionally, let it melt down completely.

Remove from the heat and split the white chocolate equally between three bowls.

Add a ¼ teaspoon pink gel food colouring to one bowl, ¼ teaspoon turquoise gel food colouring to another and leave the last bowl plain.

Fill the mermaid mould with a small amount from each of the bowls of chocolate and swirl them together gently, then leave in the freezer to set hard for 5 minutes. Carefully remove the mermaid tail from the mould and leave to one side. For the second mermaid tail, fill the mould again and freeze for another 5 minutes until set.

Place spoonfuls of each mixture in a random formation on to the baking paper then swirl the mixture together gently with a cocktail stick. Add the set chocolate mermaid tails, then scatter sprinkles and edible glitter over the top.

Leave the chocolate to set at room temperature for 45 minutes, then pop it in the fridge for 15 minutes to set hard before breaking it into shards.

The mermaid rocks are a great gift and can be wrapped in cellophane and given for a special occasion. If you're keeping them for yourself, the shards are best stored in an airtight container and kept in the fridge or at room temperature for up to 5 days – if you can make them last that long.

PARTY FOOD

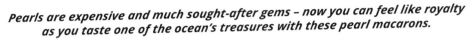

PEARL OF THE OCEAN MACARONS

Pearls are expensive and much sought-after gems – now you can feel like royalty as you taste one of the ocean's treasures with these pearl macarons.

Makes: 12 ❀ **Time: 2 hours** ❀ **Difficulty rating:** ★ ★ ★

INGREDIENTS

For the macaron shells:

* 70g ground almonds
* 140g icing sugar
* 2 large egg whites, room temperature
* Purple gel food colouring
* 50g caster sugar

For the buttercream filling:

* 100g butter, softened
* 200g icing sugar
* 1 tsp vanilla extract
* Pinch of sea salt
* 12 cream edible pearls

EXTRA EQUIPMENT

You will need a standing mixer or handheld electric whisk, two piping bags, a small round-tip piping nozzle and a small open-star piping nozzle. To decorate you will need a fine-tipped paintbrush.

METHOD

For the macaron shells:

Preheat the oven to 140–150°C, line two baking trays with baking paper and set aside.

Place the ground almonds and icing sugar in a standing mixer or use a handheld electric whisk and blitz for about a minute, then transfer to a mixing bowl.

Beat one of the egg whites into the almond and icing sugar mixture to make a smooth paste. Add a few drops purple gel food colouring and mix to fully combine, then cover the bowl with a tea towel.

Pour the second egg white into a super-clean bowl and begin to whisk on high speed to form peaks. Gradually add the caster sugar 1 tablespoon at a time, until it starts to stiffen. Once all the sugar has been added, continue beating on a high setting for 2 minutes until the mixture resembles stiff, glossy peaks.

Add the egg white mixture to the almond paste and, using a spatula, fold the two together from the bottom up. Continue that motion around 15–20 times until the mixture is fully incorporated and flows like molten lava.

Transfer the mixture into a piping bag fitted with a small round-tip nozzle and pipe 24 shell shapes on to the two lined baking trays. The mixture will spread so pipe to around 50 per cent of the size you want.

Tap the trays on a work surface a few times to release any air bubbles, then leave them to dry for 30 minutes. They will be ready to bake when they are no longer sticky or wet when touched.

Bake on the middle shelf of the oven for 8 minutes. Open the oven to let out any steam and turn the trays around, then bake for a further 8 minutes until the tops are crisp.

Leave them to cool fully before removing from the baking sheet.

Once fully cooled decorate the shells by mixing ¼ teaspoon of the purple gel food colouring with a tiny drop of water to help thin the food colouring. Paint thin lines down the shells to replicate the ridges.

For the buttercream:
Cream together the butter and icing sugar until smooth and fluffy.

Add the vanilla extract and sea salt and mix through to combine.

Transfer to a piping bag fitted with a small open-star nozzle and pipe the buttercream on to one half of the macaron shells. Rest an edible pearl on the buttercream towards the front of the macarons and top with the remaining macaron shells. Leave in the fridge for 30 minutes before serving.

These will store in an airtight container for a few days if kept in the fridge.

🐚 CORAL REEF ECLAIRS 🐚

These colourful delights will transport you to an underwater world teeming with friendly fish and vibrant reefs.

Makes: 8 🐚 Time: 1 hour 🐚 Difficulty rating: ★ ★

INGREDIENTS

For the choux pastry:

* 125ml water
* 50g unsalted butter, chilled
* 65g plain flour, sifted
* Pinch of salt
* 2 eggs, lightly whisked

For the filling and topping:

* 200ml whipping cream
* 1 tsp vanilla extract
* 400g icing sugar
* 200g white chocolate, broken into squares
* 200g butter, softened
* Gel food colouring (pink, orange and green)

EXTRA EQUIPMENT

You will need five piping bags, a 1cm round nozzle, three closed-star nozzles and a chopstick.

METHOD

For the choux pastry:

Preheat the oven to 200°C and line a baking tray with baking paper.

Place the water and butter in a saucepan over a low heat and cook until the butter melts. Increase the heat to medium-high and bring the mixture to a boil.

Remove the pan from the heat and use a wooden spoon to beat in the flour and salt until well combined. Place the pan over a low heat and continue cooking, stirring with a wooden spoon constantly for 30 seconds or until the mixture comes away from the sides of the pan.

Set aside for 5 minutes to cool a little then gradually beat in half the whisked egg. Repeat with the remaining egg, beating until the mixture is thick and glossy.

Transfer the dough mixture to a piping bag fitted with a 1cm-round nozzle. Pipe ten 12cm-long lines on to the lined tray and bake in the oven for 20–25 minutes or until the eclairs are puffed and golden.

Insert a hole into one end of the eclair using a chopstick then bake in the oven for a further 5 minutes. Transfer to a wire rack to cool completely.

For the filling and topping:

Whip the cream with 5 tablespoons of icing sugar and 1 teaspoon of vanilla extract in a bowl until stiff.

Fill a piping bag fitted with a small round-tip nozzle and pipe in the whipped cream through the hole you created at one end of the éclair.

For the white chocolate glaze, melt the chocolate in a heatproof bowl set over a pan of simmering water. Once the chocolate has melted dip the tops of the eclairs in the chocolate and let the chocolate set.

To make the buttercream, mix the butter and the rest of the icing sugar together until combined and fluffy. Split the mixture between three bowls and add a good few drops to each (so one bowl is pink, one orange and one green). Fill three piping bags with the different coloured buttercream and fit them with the closed-star nozzles. Pipe random peaks of the buttercream on top of the eclairs then serve.

🐚 SHARK TEETH KEBABS 🐚

These kebabs certainly don't bite but they do pack a punch.

Makes: 4 🐚 **Time: 30 minutes** 🐚 **Difficulty rating:** ⭐

INGREDIENTS

* ½ watermelon
* 4 kiwi fruits
* 8–10 strawberries, hulled
* 8–10 blueberries

EXTRA EQUIPMENT

You will need four kebab skewers.

METHOD

Slice the watermelon into 2cm-thick slices and remove the flesh from the skin.

Cut out four 5cm square cubes from the watermelon, then cut them diagonally in half to create triangles and set aside.

Peel and thickly slice the kiwi fruits into eight pieces then cut them into triangle shapes and set aside.

Slice the strawberries in half lengthways and set aside.

Assemble by piercing a piece of watermelon, followed by two blueberries, then a strawberry, then a kiwi fruit on to a kebab skewer.

Repeat this step to fill the kebab skewer.

Continue with the remaining skewers and serve the fruit kebabs on their own or with a pot of melted chocolate for dipping.

⚜ MERMAID MARSHMALLOW ⚜ CRISPY BARS

Get nostalgic with these crispy bars, which are made from all your favourite childhood indulgences.

Makes: 8 ⚜ **Time: 1 hour 30 minutes** ⚜ **Difficulty rating:** ★

INGREDIENTS

- ★ 50g butter
- ★ 200g mini marshmallows
- ★ 125g puffed rice
- ★ 200g white chocolate
- ★ Turquoise gel food colouring
- ★ Edible flower cupcake toppers
- ★ Edible pearl sprinkles
- ★ Edible glitter

EXTRA EQUIPMENT

You will need a 20cm square baking tin.

METHOD

Grease the baking tin and set aside.

Put the butter and marshmallows into a large pan and melt together on the hob over a medium heat.

Once melted, add the puffed rice and mix together until well coated.

Transfer the sticky mixture into the greased baking tray, spread it out into all corners and flatten the top. Leave to set for 1 hour at room temperature.

Once set, tip the baking tray upside down and tap the bottom until the mixture falls out, then cut it into eight equal squares.

To decorate, melt the white chocolate in a heatproof bowl set over a pan of simmering water. Add a drop of the turquoise gel food colouring and stir it through until you have a mint green colour. Leave it to cool for 5 minutes.

Dip the marshmallow squares halfway into the chocolate and lay them out on a baking tray lined with baking paper. Leave to set in the fridge for 10 minutes, then repeat for a second coat.

Top with edible pearl sprinkles and a dusting of edible glitter then, with a little remaining white chocolate, stick the sugar flowers above the dipped white chocolate to resemble the mermaid bikini.

🐚 PEARL CAKE POPS 🐚

Smooth and silky, these cake pops reflect what pearls would taste like if they were edible.

Makes: 20 🐚 **Time: 1–2 hours** 🐚 **Difficulty rating:** ⭐

INGREDIENTS

For the cake:

* ★ 120g butter, softened
* ★ 150g caster sugar
* ★ 180g self-raising flour
* ★ 4 tbsp milk
* ★ 2 eggs
* ★ 1 tsp vanilla extract

For the icing:

* ★ 80g butter, softened
* ★ 1 tsp vanilla extract
* ★ 40g cream cheese, softened
* ★ 200g icing sugar, sifted

For the decorations:

* ★ 500g melted white chocolate
* ★ 1 tsp vegetable oil
* ★ Blue and green gel food colouring
* ★ 100g icing sugar
* ★ Edible silver glitter

EXTRA EQUIPMENT

You will need 20 lollipop sticks and a cake-pop stand.

METHOD

For the cake:

Preheat the oven to 180°C and line a 20cm cake tin and a baking tray with baking paper.

Place the butter, sugar, flour, milk, eggs and vanilla into a bowl and beat together for 2–3 minutes until smooth, pale and fluffy.

Pour the mixture into the pre-prepared tin, bake for 35–40 minutes and leave the cake to cool on a wire rack.

For the icing:

Cream the butter, vanilla and cream cheese together until smooth and gradually add the icing sugar, then continue to mix until light and fluffy. Refrigerate for 30 minutes.

For the cake pops:

Crumble the cooled sponge in a large mixing bowl with your hands until you have fine crumbs.

Add heaped tablespoons of the cream cheese icing and begin mixing it in with the crumbs. You may not require all the icing as it will depend on how moist your sponge is. Keep mixing and adding the icing until you have a fudge-like texture that doesn't crumble when squeezed between your hands.

Wrap the mixture in cling film and chill for at least 1 hour to firm up.

Once chilled, break off small pieces of the mixture (about the size of a ping-pong ball) and roll them into balls with your hands. You want to make 20 balls in total. Place each ball on the lined baking tray and put it in the fridge for 15–20 minutes.

For the decorations:

Melt the white chocolate in a heatproof bowl set over a pan of simmering water then mix in 1 teaspoon of vegetable oil. This will make the melted chocolate smoother and easier to coat the cake pops with.

Split the chocolate into two bowls, and add a few drops of the blue gel food colouring to one and a few drops of green gel food colouring to the other. Mix both and, if necessary, add more food colouring until you have a bowl of vibrant blue chocolate and a bowl of vibrant green chocolate.

To assemble the cake pops, dip the lollipop sticks into either the blue or green melted chocolate one at a time and then push each of them into the middle of one of the cake pops. (Dipping the sticks into the chocolate first will help secure them to the cake balls.) Then dip the entire surface of the cake pops into your desired chocolate (green or blue) until fully coated, making sure you hold them upside down for a few seconds to let the excess chocolate drip off. Once they are coated with chocolate, place them in the cake-pop stand and sprinkle edible glitter on to half of the blue cake pops. Chill all the cake pops in the fridge or in a cool room for 1 hour.

Meanwhile, mix the icing sugar and a few teaspoons of water in a large bowl until you have a ribbon consistency that leaves a visible trail behind for a short while when mixed.

Split the mixture into two bowls and colour one bowl blue and leave the other bright white.

When the cake pops are set, drizzle the white icing over the blue cake pops that aren't covered in edible glitter and leave them upside down on a plate.

Then drizzle blue and white icing over the green cake pops and leave them aside on the plate upside down to set completely before serving.

🐚 OCTOPUS ARM CHURROS 🐚

Did you know that an octopus can regrow its arms? If you end up eating all these churros, be like an octopus and make some more!

Makes: 8 🐚 Time: 2 hours 🐚 Difficulty rating: ⭐ ⭐

INGREDIENTS

For the churros:

* ⋆ 50g butter, melted
* ⋆ ½ tsp vanilla extract
* ⋆ 250g plain flour
* ⋆ 1 tsp baking powder
* ⋆ 1 litre sunflower oil
* ⋆ 100g caster sugar
* ⋆ 2 tsp cinnamon

For the chocolate sauce:

* ⋆ 200g dark chocolate
* ⋆ 100ml double cream
* ⋆ 100ml whole milk
* ⋆ 3 tbsp golden syrup
* ⋆ ½ tsp vanilla extract

EXTRA EQUIPMENT

You will need a large piping bag, a 2cm open-star piping nozzle, a large deep saucepan and two baking trays.

METHOD

For the churro dough:

Measure 350ml boiling water into a jug and add the melted butter and vanilla extract.

Sift the flour and baking powder into a large mixing bowl, then make a well in the centre and pour in the butter and water mixture, beating it into the flour quickly with a wooden spoon until lump-free. Leave to stand for 10–15 minutes.

For the chocolate sauce:

Put all the sauce ingredients into a pan and gently melt them together, stirring until you have a smooth shiny sauce. Keep warm on a low heat, stirring occasionally.

Frying the churros:

(*Safety note: cooking with hot oil can be dangerous and safety instructions should be followed to avoid accidents. Before frying, ensure young children are kept away from the pan and you are protected by wearing long sleeves. Never leave a pan of oil heating on a stove unattended. Use a large sturdy pan and keep the pan's handles away from the front of the cooker to avoid knocking it*

off the hob. While frying, keep your eyes away from the pan in case the oil spits at you. Have a large slotted spoon or sturdy tongs ready to lift out the churros.)

Prepare the two baking trays by lining one with baking paper and spreading the caster sugar and cinnamon on the other, mixing them together to form a cinnamon sugar.

Fit a large piping bag with the open-star piping nozzle and fill it with the dough, then set aside.

Fill a large deep pan with sunflower oil so that it is no more than two-thirds full.

Heat it until it reaches 180°C then pipe 2–3 strips about 10–15cm long directly into the pan, snipping off each dough strip with a pair of kitchen scissors. (*Note: be extra careful when adding the dough to the hot oil.*)

Fry for 45 seconds to 1 minute until golden brown and crisp then remove with a slotted spoon or tongs and drain on the lined baking tray.

Add your next batch of churro strips into the oil, then return to the cooked churros and roll them in the cinnamon sugar.

Continue the process until all churros are cooked and coated, then serve with the chocolate sauce for dipping.

These are best eaten immediately.

🐚 SEABED ROCKY ROAD 🐚

Just like a seabed, this rocky road has lots of hidden gems in it.

Makes: 12 🐚 **Time: 1 hour 30 minutes** 🐚 **Difficulty rating:** ⭐

INGREDIENTS

* 200g chocolate digestive biscuits
* 135g butter
* 100g dark chocolate
* 100g milk chocolate
* 2–3 tbsp golden syrup
* 100g mini marshmallows
* 50g glacé cherries
* Sweets to decorate
* Icing sugar to dust

EXTRA EQUIPMENT

You will need a square 20cm baking tin.

METHOD

Line the baking tin with baking paper and set aside.

Place the biscuits into a freezer bag and crush with a rolling pin until you have a mixture of fine crumbs and larger pieces. Set aside.

In a large pan, melt the butter, chocolate and golden syrup over a medium heat, stirring until completely melted.

Remove the pan from the heat, then add the biscuits, marshmallows and glacé cherries and stir it all together until everything is coated.

Pour the mixture into the prepared baking tin and spread it out evenly into all the corners, then top with the sweets.

Leave in the fridge for 1 hour to set then dust with a little icing sugar and cut into 12 equal squares.

❧ PERSONALISED MERMAID ❧ TAIL BISCUITS

Did you know that the colour of a mermaid's tail depicts her mood and personality? Now you can create your own customised mermaid tail, coloured and designed to reflect your very own mermaid personality.

Makes: 15 ❧ **Time: 2 hours** ❧ **Difficulty rating:** ★ ★

INGREDIENTS

For the biscuits:

* ★ 85g unsalted butter
* ★ 100g golden caster sugar
* ★ 1 egg
* ★ ½ tsp vanilla extract
* ★ 200g plain flour, plus more for dusting
* ★ ¼ tsp salt
* ★ ½ tsp baking powder

For the icing:

* ★ 900g royal icing sugar
* ★ 150ml cold water
* ★ A variety of gel food colourings

EXTRA EQUIPMENT

You will need two baking trays, baking paper, a rolling pin, a mermaid tail cookie cutter, several piping bags, a writing-tip piping nozzle and cocktail sticks.

METHOD

For the biscuits:

Preheat the oven to 180°C and line two baking trays with baking paper.

Put the butter and sugar in a bowl and cream together with a wooden spoon until smooth, then add the egg and vanilla extract and mix well. Gradually add the flour, salt and baking powder, and mix to combine into a dough.

On a floured work surface, roll the dough out to a thickness of about 5mm, then cut out your mermaid tails with your cutter. You will need to reroll the leftover dough a few times to be able to cut out all 15 biscuits.

Place the tails on the baking trays, ensuring they are well spaced out to allow for a little spreading, then bake for about 10–12 minutes, until light golden brown.

Leave to cool on a wire rack. If you want to make the biscuits ahead of icing them, they will keep for 2–3 days in an airtight container stored at room temperature.

For the different icing techniques:

Pour 150ml cold water into a large bowl and add all the royal icing sugar.

Combine the two together, slowly at first to avoid a sugar cloud, then beat for around 5 minutes until the mixture is bright, white and the consistency of toothpaste.

Divide into bowls and colour each to your desired tone.

Line icing:

Line icing should be the texture of toothpaste.

To line your biscuits fit a piping bag with a writing-tip piping nozzle and fill it with your desired icing colour. Pipe around the edges of your mermaid tails, making sure that you join up your trail to form an unbroken wall, and let the walls dry for about 5 minutes.

If you want to add any detail, such as the blue mermaid scales design, keep some of your line icing back so you can pipe this on after you've filled your biscuits.

Flood icing:

Flood icing is a runnier consistency and is used to fill the space in between the line icing. To create flood icing mix a little bit of water into the line icing to create a slightly looser consistency.

Tip: don't add too much in one go; take it a few drops at a time to ensure you don't add too much and consequently ruin the icing.

You can pipe the flood icing using a squeeze piping bottle or a piping bag, just simply fill them with the icing and carefully fill the area you wish to colour. Don't add too much as you can spread it out with a cocktail stick. If you fill too much it could overflow the lines.

Leave the icing to dry for 30 minutes before serving.

Wet on wet:

The polka-dot mermaid tail design was created using the wet-on-wet technique.

To create this, once you have flooded your biscuits, simply add a tiny drop of another colour straight on to the wet icing, using a cocktail stick or a piping bag fitted with a writing-tip nozzle, and watch it merge together.

Marble:

For the marble technique simply flood the biscuits with two or three different colours and mix the colours together with a cocktail stick to create the marble effect.

❀ MESMERISING MADELEINES ❀

Charm your taste buds with these simple, delicious and light madeleines.

Makes: 12　❀　Time: 45 minutes　❀　Difficulty rating: ★

INGREDIENTS

- ★ 100g butter, melted (plus a little extra for preparing the tray)
- ★ 100g plain flour (plus a little extra for preparing the tray)
- ★ 2 eggs
- ★ 100g caster sugar
- ★ Juice and zest of 1 lemon
- ★ ¾ tsp baking powder
- ★ Icing sugar, for dusting

EXTRA EQUIPMENT

You will need a madeleine tray and a pastry brush.

METHOD

Preheat the oven to 200°C and brush the madeleine tray with melted butter. Sprinkle in a little flour to coat and tap out any excess then set aside.

Whisk together the eggs and the sugar in a bowl until frothy, then gradually add the butter, lemon juice and zest, followed by the flour and baking powder, whisking them all in as they are added.

Leave to stand for 20 minutes before carefully pouring the mixture into the prepared madeleine tray. Bake for 8–10 minutes then transfer to a wire rack and leave for a few minutes to cool slightly. Dust lightly with icing sugar and eat within an hour of baking for the best taste experience.

🐚 JELLYFISH LAYERED SURPRISE 🐚

Just before you serve this fruity dessert, salute the jellyfish that inspired it with a jiggle and a wiggle.

Serves: 10–12 🐚 Time: 3 hours 🐚 Difficulty rating: ⭐

INGREDIENTS

* ★ Oil for greasing
* ★ ½ pack blackcurrant jelly
* ★ 2½ packs gelatine powder
* ★ 397g condensed milk
* ★ ½ pack orange jelly
* ★ 1 pack raspberry jelly
* ★ 800ml boiling water
* ★ 300ml cold water

EXTRA EQUIPMENT

You will need a 1lb loaf tin and four mixing bowls.

METHOD

Grease a 1lb loaf tin with a little oil and set aside.

In one mixing bowl, add ½ pack blackcurrant jelly to ½ a pack of gelatine powder and pour over 250ml of boiling water. Stir it through until the jelly cubes have melted then pour into the prepared loaf tin and chill in the fridge for 15–30 minutes.

Meanwhile prepare the next layer by stirring together the condensed milk and 100ml of boiling water.

In a separate bowl, combine 100ml cold water and ½ a pack of gelatine powder and allow the mixture to set for 2–3 minutes. Once set, pour the gelatine into the condensed milk and combine. Set aside at room temperature for later.

In a fourth bowl, add ½ a pack of gelatine powder, ½ a pack of orange jelly and 100ml of cold water, and let it sit for 5 minutes. Then add 100ml of boiling water and stir it through until the jelly cubes have dissolved. Let the mixture cool a little then add half of the creamy condensed milk mixture to it and combine to make a light creamy yellow colour.

Pour this layer over the set blackcurrant jelly and chill in the fridge for 15–30 minutes.

For the next layer, add ½ a pack of raspberry jelly with ½ a pack of gelatine powder to a bowl and pour over 250ml of boiling water.

Stir it through until the jelly cubes have dissolved, then pour on top of the set creamy yellow layer and chill for 15–30 minutes.

In another bowl, add ½ a pack of gelatine powder, the remaining ½ pack of raspberry jelly and 100ml of cold water, and let it sit for 5 minutes. Then add 100ml of boiling water and stir it through until the jelly cubes have dissolved. Let the mixture cool a little and then add the remaining half of the creamy condensed milk mixture to it, combining to make a light pink colour.

Pour this layer over the set raspberry jelly layer and chill in the fridge for a final 30 minutes.

To serve, cut around the edge of the jelly to loosen a little, then carefully turn it out on to a serving dish and cut into slices.

BREAKFAST

🐚 MERMAID TOAST 🐚

*Start your morning off with a colourful breakfast – it will
keep you smiling for the rest of the day!*

Serves: 2 🐚 Time: 15 minutes 🐚 Difficulty rating: ★

INGREDIENTS

- ★ 250g cream cheese
- ★ Pink and turquoise gel food colouring
- ★ 2 slices of white bread
- ★ Handful of raspberries
- ★ 2–3 slices of watermelon

EXTRA EQUIPMENT

You will need a 1cm star cutter.

METHOD

Split the cream cheese between two bowls and add a drop of pink gel food colouring to one bowl and a drop of turquoise gel food colouring to the other to create pastel tones.

Toast two slices of white bread and then leave to cool slightly.

While the toast cools cut out four (or more if desired) watermelon stars using a 1cm star cutter and leave to one side.

Add 2 teaspoons of the pink cream cheese to the top left half of the toast and 2 teaspoons of the turquoise cream cheese to the bottom right half.

Using a butter knife, spread the mixture across to cover the toast at a diagonal angle. When the two colours meet, blend them together and then top with the watermelon stars and a few raspberries. Repeat these steps for the second piece of toast.

🐚 STARFISH PANCAKES 🐚

A starfish a day keeps the sea doctor away, so the mermaids say. Whether or not this legend is true, these starfish pancakes will certainly give you a boost of energy.

Makes: 8 🐚 Time: 20 minutes 🐚 Difficulty rating: ★

INGREDIENTS

For the grapefruit syrup:

* ★ Zest of 2 pink grapefruits
* ★ 140g caster sugar
* ★ 230ml water

For the pancakes:

* ★ 150g plain flour
* ★ ½ tsp salt
* ★ 1 tbsp baking powder
* ★ 1 tbsp caster sugar
* ★ 225ml milk
* ★ 1 egg
* ★ 1 tsp butter or oil for frying
* ★ Orange and yellow gel food colouring

For the decoration:

* ★ Grapefruit slices
* ★ Pomegranate seeds

EXTRA EQUIPMENT

You will need one large and one medium-sized star cookie cutter.

METHOD

For the grapefruit syrup:

Wash the grapefruits under cold water and dry before grating the peel finely until you have one heaped tablespoon.

Add the sugar and zest to a bowl and mix using the back of a wooden spoon, crushing the zest into the sugar until the sugar looks damp. Cover well and let sit for 30 minutes.

Bring the water to a boil in a medium saucepan and stir in the citrus sugar. Simmer the sugar for 3 minutes until it's all dissolved.

Take off the heat and it let cool a little before straining out the zest and decanting the syrup into a sterilised jar or bottle.

For the pancakes:

Preheat the oven to 100ºC, then sift together the flour, salt and baking powder in a large bowl, and add the caster sugar. Make a well in the centre, pour in the milk, then add the egg and whisk until the pancake batter is smooth.

Divide the mixture between two bowls and add ¼ teaspoon of orange gel food colouring to one and ¼ teaspoon of yellow gel food colouring to the other, mixing them through to combine.

Pour the orange mixture into a measuring jug and heat a large frying pan over a medium heat.

Add a knob of butter, leave it to melt and then pour in two circles of pancake batter large enough to cut star shapes out of.

Cook each pancake until bubbles appear on the surface, then flip them over with a spatula and cook for 20–30 seconds on the reverse side. You don't want to brown them too much or you'll lose the colour.

Set aside the cooked pancakes on a plate and leave in a warm oven then repeat with two more rounds of the orange pancake batter. Once all the orange pancakes are cooked, begin frying the yellow pancake batter.

When all the pancakes are cooked, use a large star-shaped cookie cutter to cut out star shapes from the orange pancake batter and then use the medium star-shaped cookie cutter for the yellow pancakes.

Serve warm with a dash of grapefruit syrup, a slice of fresh grapefruit and pomegranate seeds.

🐚 TROPICAL SEA SMOOTHIE BOWL 🐚

Plunge into the tropical seas with this delicious coconut and banana bowl.

Serves: 2 🐚 Time: 15 minutes 🐚 Difficulty rating: ★

INGREDIENTS

For the decorations:

- ★ ½ papaya
- ★ 2 kiwi fruits
- ★ 2 tbsp shredded coconut
- ★ Handful of blueberries
- ★ Squeeze of lemon

For the smoothie mixture:

- ★ 4 bananas
- ★ 200ml coconut milk
- ★ ¼ tsp spirulina powder
- ★ Handful of ice

EXTRA EQUIPMENT

You will need a blender, a 1cm star cutter and a 2cm flower cutter.

METHOD

For the decorations:

Using the star cutter, cut the papaya into ten star shapes and set aside. Then cut the kiwi fruit into ten flower shapes. Squeeze a little bit of lemon juice over the fruit to keep it fresh and put to one side.

For the smoothie mixture:

Put the bananas, coconut milk, spirulina powder and ice into a blender and blitz until smooth. It will take a few pulses to break down the ice.

Split the mixture between two bowls then lay the kiwi fruit flowers out in a row on one side, followed by the papaya stars, the shredded coconut and finally the blueberries.

🐚 TURTLE WAFFLES 🐚

These waffles will help you to be more turtle: cool, calm and collected, duuuuude.

Makes: 6 🐚 **Time: 1 hour 30 minutes** 🐚 **Difficulty rating: ★**

INGREDIENTS

For the waffles:

* ★ 100ml milk
* ★ 1 tsp active dried yeast
* ★ 1 tsp soft light brown sugar, or more to taste
* ★ 120g flour
* ★ 1 tsp cornflour
* ★ ¼ tsp salt
* ★ 120ml buttermilk
* ★ 2 tbsp butter, melted
* ★ 1 small egg, beaten
* ★ Oil, to grease

For the decorations:

* ★ 6 bananas (1 per waffle)
* ★ 200g blueberries
* ★ Honey, maple syrup or chocolate to drizzle
* ★ 12 edible eyes

EXTRA EQUIPMENT

You will need an electronic circular waffle maker.

METHOD

For the waffles:

Warm the milk in a small pan on a low heat until warm enough to hold your finger in, then remove from the heat and stir in the yeast followed by a pinch of the sugar and leave for 5 minutes or so until the surface is covered with tiny bubbles.

Meanwhile, whisk together the remaining sugar, both flours and salt in a large bowl and set aside. Then, in a jug, beat together the buttermilk, melted butter and egg.

Whisk the yeast and milk mixture into the jug, then slowly pour this into the bowl of dry ingredients, mixing gently with a large spoon. Cover loosely with cling film and allow to sit at room temperature for an hour.

Turn the oven on low to help keep the waffles you cook warm. Lightly grease then heat your waffle iron.

Pour just enough batter into your waffle maker to cover the base, spreading it out with a metal spatula or palette knife, then turn down the heat slightly and close the lid. Cook for about 45 seconds until golden on the underside, then flip and leave for about 4 minutes until that side is golden and crisp. Repeat this process until you have cooked all six waffles.

For the decorations:

For each waffle, peel a banana and cut off one end for the turtle head, then position two edible eyes at the tip.

Cut off the other end of the banana leaving the mid-section about 3cm long. Take the end section of the banana and cut it in half lengthways. Then cut the flat end of each half at a slight angle and position one either side of the waffle for their fins, with the banana tips pointing out.

Then take the 3cm mid-section, cut it in half and shape each piece into a slight point. Position one each side at the bottom of the waffle for the turtle feet.

Decorate with blueberries and a splash of honey, maple syrup or chocolate and eat immediately while still warm.

DESSERTS

🐚 MERMAID CHEESECAKE 🐚

*Give an ordinary ginger and lime cheesecake a mystical
mermaid twist with this beautiful jelly topping.*

Serves: 10 🐚 **Time: 5 hours (in stages)** 🐚 **Difficulty rating: ⭐ ⭐ ⭐**

INGREDIENTS

For the base:

* 150g digestive biscuits
* 100g ginger biscuits
* 100g butter, melted

For the cheesecake filling:

* 300g cream cheese, full fat
* 200g mascarpone
* 100g icing sugar
* Juice and zest of 1 lime
* 2 drops vanilla extract
* 230ml double cream

For the scales:

* 250g white fondant icing
* Blue and green gel
  food colouring

For the jelly topping:

* 275ml water
* 8g powdered gelatine
* 1 tbsp sugar
* Blue and green gel
  food colouring

EXTRA EQUIPMENT

You will need a 20cm springform tin, a 3cm circular cutter (or a
large bottle top) and a cocktail stick (optional).

METHOD

For the base:

Grease your tin lightly with butter and line the base (but not the
sides) with a circle of baking paper.

Place the biscuits in a sealable food bag and crush them into fine
crumbs with a rolling pin. You may need to do this in batches if
your bag is small.

Put the crumbs in a bowl. Melt the butter, add this to the biscuit
crumbs and stir thoroughly so that the crumbs are evenly coated.
Tip the mixture into the tin and press down firmly with the back
of a spoon so that an even layer is formed. Be sure to push the
mixture to the edges so that there are no gaps. Chill in the fridge
for at least an hour.

For the cheesecake filling:

Put the cream cheese, mascarpone, icing sugar, lime juice, lime
zest and vanilla extract in a large bowl and beat with an electric
whisk until smooth.

In a smaller bowl, whip the double cream by hand with a whisk or
a fork until it is thick and smooth. It should hold soft peaks when
you lift the whisk from the bowl. Then add it to the cream cheese
mixture and stir until completely combined.

Take the base from the fridge. Spoon the cheesecake mixture on to the base and smooth it into an even layer with the back of a dessert spoon. Ensure that you push the mixture into the edges so that you don't have any air bubbles. Leave to set in the fridge for 4 hours or overnight.

For the scales:

Divide the fondant into five equal portions of 50g each. Take the first portion of fondant and add one small drop each of blue and green gel food colouring. Fold the fondant to mix the colour in. Set aside once you have achieved a pale green-blue colour.

Do this for the remaining portions of fondant, adding slightly more colour each time so that each portion is slightly darker than the last.

Dust a clean surface with icing sugar. Roll out one of the fondant portions until it is no more than 2mm thick (the thinner you can get it, the better). Cut out circles with the cutter and put them to one side. Re-roll the offcuts of fondant as many times as you need.

To make the scale shape, take the same cutter you used to cut out the circle. Cut out the top left and right quarters of the circle with the edge of the cutter. To keep your scales consistent, you could draw out a template on baking paper for this step. You may also need to cut off the very tip of the scale for the scales to fit together evenly.

Draw a circle the same size as your cheesecake on to a sheet of baking paper and lay out the scales from light to dark as they will appear on the cheesecake. You will have to cut some to size so that they fit around the edges. Then leave them uncovered for 3–4 hours to dry out. Once the scales are dry, begin making the jelly.

For the jelly and assembly:

Heat 65ml of water until it is hot but not boiling and put it in a small bowl or jug. Sprinkle the gelatine over the hot water. (*Note: for the gelatine to dissolve properly it is important that it's added to the water and not the other way around.*)

Stir until the gelatine has completely dissolved. If the gelatine does not dissolve completely after a minute or so, put the bowl or jug in a pan of warm water to heat it gently and continue to stir. Once dissolved, put to one side. Stir it occasionally to ensure it doesn't set.

Heat 210ml of water in a small pan until it is hot but not boiling. Add the sugar and stir until dissolved. Turn the heat to low, add the gelatine mixture and stir to combine.

Transfer to a heatproof jug and add a small amount of both gel food colourings to turn the mixture a pale blue-green. Leave the mixture to cool for a few minutes, stirring occasionally to ensure that it doesn't set.

While the jelly is cooling, transfer the fondant mermaid scales to the cheesecake. A cocktail stick can be helpful to make small adjustments to the scales' positioning.

Once the jelly is lukewarm to the touch it is ready. Use a dessert spoon to place it on to the top of the cheesecake. Do this gently so as not to displace the scales. Once you have a thin covering of jelly over the whole cheesecake transfer it to the fridge. (*Note: you probably won't need all the jelly mixture.*) Leave for 4–6 hours, or overnight, to set.

Once the jelly has set, remove the cheesecake gently from the tin. Bring to room temperature to serve.

🐚 SEAFOAM MOUSSE 🐚

Whip up this creamy dessert for your guests and watch them savour every mouthful!

Serves: 4 🐚 **Time: 15 minutes** 🐚 **Difficulty rating:** ⭐

INGREDIENTS

* ½ tsp gelatine powder
* 30ml cold water
* 350ml double cream
* 200g icing sugar
* 500g cream cheese
* ½ tsp peppermint extract
* Green gel food colouring
* 200g dark chocolate (minimum 70 per cent cocoa), finely chopped
* Whipped cream, in a can
* Two squares dark chocolate to garnish
* Fresh mint leaves to garnish

METHOD

Add the gelatine to a small bowl with 30ml water and leave it to one side for 5–10 minutes.

Pour the double cream into a large bowl and whip until it forms soft peaks, then add 30g of the icing sugar and whip until it forms stiff peaks. (*Note: be careful not to overbeat your cream as it will split.*)

In another bowl, add the cream cheese and mix it with an electric whisk until smooth and fluffy, then add the remaining icing sugar and mix it through until combined.

Add the peppermint extract and a drop of green gel food colouring to the cream cheese mix to give you a light, mint-green tone, and mix them both through.

Heat up the set gelatine in a microwave on full power or in a small pan on a medium heat for no longer than 30 seconds, then remove and whisk to ensure it dissolves. Let it cool slightly for 2 minutes, then pour the gelatine mixture into the cream cheese mixture and blend it through thoroughly with the electric whisk.

Add the cream and sugar mixture and almost all of the finely chopped chocolate, and gently fold it through until evenly combined. Spoon the mixture into your serving dishes. Use large wine glasses, or any glass or serving dishes suitable. Chill in the fridge for 3 hours or overnight.

Pipe the canned whipped cream over the top and garnish with fresh mint leaves, two squares of chocolate and the remaining chopped chocolate to serve.

🐚 UNDER THE SEA ICE LOLLIES 🐚

Cool down on a hot summer's day with these refreshing and fizzy frozen treats.

Makes: 4 🐚 **Time: 15 minutes** 🐚 **Difficulty rating:** ⭐

INGREDIENTS

* ★ 1 kiwi fruit
* ★ Handful blueberries
* ★ 200ml lemonade
* ★ Turquoise gel food colouring

EXTRA EQUIPMENT

You will need a four-hole ice lolly mould and four ice lolly sticks.

METHOD

Cut the kiwi fruit into thin slices and stick one slice on to one side of each ice lolly mould, then put some blueberries at the bottom of the moulds.

Put the moulds into the freezer so the fruit freezes against the sides.

Pour the lemonade into a jug, add a drop of the turquoise gel food colouring and stir.

Remove the moulds from the freezer and fill each with the blue lemonade.

Position a lolly stick in the centre of each lolly mould then put them back in the freezer.

The lolly sticks will rise with the bubbles, but after 20 minutes when the mixture has begun to set you can readjust them and then leave the mixture to freeze completely.

To remove the lollies, warm up the moulds with your hands and gently twist and pull the lollies up and out.

Eat immediately.

☙ TROPICAL SWISS ROLL ☙

Dig out the deckchairs, play some calypso music and feel fully relaxed as you enjoy this slice of food paradise.

Serves: 6–8 ☙ Time: 2 hours ☙ Difficulty rating: ★ ★

INGREDIENTS

For the sponge:

* 3 eggs
* 75g caster sugar (plus 2 tbsp extra for dusting)
* 75g plain flour
* Zest of 1 lime

For the lime curd filling:

* 100g caster sugar
* 25g butter
* 2 eggs, lightly beaten
* Juice of 2 limes
* Zest of 1 lime
* 400ml can full-fat coconut milk, chilled in the fridge and unshaken
* ½ tsp vanilla extract
* 85g icing sugar

For the decorations:

* Lime zest
* Coconut flakes

EXTRA EQUIPMENT

You will need a Swiss roll tin or a 25cm x 37cm shallow baking tin and a palette knife.

METHOD

For the sponge:

Preheat the oven to 170°C and line a Swiss roll tin or a shallow baking tin with baking paper.

In a large bowl, whisk together the eggs and caster sugar for around 5 minutes until the mixture is pale, thick and the consistency is like mousse.

Sift the flour and add the zest into the mixture and gently fold them in – take your time with this as you don't want to lose any air.

Spread the mixture out into the lined tin using a palette knife and bake for 8–10 minutes. Remove when it is a pale golden colour and slightly springy. Leave to cool for 5 minutes.

When it is cool enough to touch, sprinkle an extra 2 tablespoons of caster sugar over a fresh sheet of baking paper and quickly flip the cake on to the paper, peeling the lining paper away from the cooked sponge.

While it is still warm, carefully roll the sponge (from the short end) using the baking paper as support to lift it, then leave to cool in the rolled-up position.

For the filling:

Put the sugar, butter, eggs and lime juice into a pan and melt together over a medium heat.

Simmer the mixture gently for around 10–15 minutes, whisking frequently, until it becomes a thick curd.

Pour the curd through a sieve into a bowl, then stir in the lime zest and leave to cool.

To make the coconut cream, scoop the chilled coconut cream from the top of the can of coconut milk into a bowl and leave the liquid behind. Add the vanilla extract and icing sugar, and mix until creamy and smooth.

To assemble the Swiss roll:

When the sponge has fully cooled, unroll it and smooth out a layer of half the coconut cream on top, followed by a layer of the lime curd.

Gently re-roll the sponge and then smooth the remaining coconut cream across the top and down the sides.

Finish with a sprinkle of coconut flakes and lime zest, then cut the ends off to neaten and transfer to a serving plate. Eat within 24 hours.

🐚 CORAL FRUIT TARTS 🐚

One taste of these tarts and you'll be transported to a tropical paradise. If the rain pattering on your window is denying you this vision, just imagine you're a mermaid swimming in the sea.

Makes: 12   🐚   Time: 2 hours   🐚   Difficulty rating: ★ ★

INGREDIENTS

For the tart cases:

* 100g butter, cold
* 175g plain flour
* 2 tbsp icing sugar
* 1 egg, beaten

For the filling:

* 100g caster sugar
* 250g cream cheese
* 1 tsp vanilla
* 250ml double cream
* Fresh fruit (kiwi, mango, raspberries and blueberries)

EXTRA EQUIPMENT

You will need a mini cupcake tin, a 5cm flower cookie cutter, a rolling pin, a 1cm star cutter, a piping bag, a round-tip piping nozzle and baking beans or rice.

METHOD

For the tart cases:

Preheat the oven to 180°C.

Put the butter and flour in a bowl and mix together with your fingers to create breadcrumbs.

Add the icing sugar and stir it through, then add the egg and bring the mixture together to form a dough.

Roll the dough out to a thickness of approximately 1cm, then cut out shapes using the flower cookie cutter and repeat until you have 12 flower shapes.

Gently press the shapes into the mini cupcake tin holes, and fill each with a small square of baking paper and a few baking beans (alternatively you can fill with uncooked rice).

Bake for 10–15 minutes, checking regularly, until the tarts are lightly golden, then remove from the oven, take out the baking beans/rice and cool on a wire rack.

For the filling:

In a large bowl beat the sugar, cream cheese and vanilla together for 2–3 minutes until creamy.

In another bowl whip the double cream and then fold it into the cheesecake mixture.

Transfer the mixture to a piping bag, fitted with a round-tip nozzle, and fill each tart case with a generous amount.

Top the tarts with sliced kiwi, star-shaped mango pieces, blueberries and raspberries, and serve.

You can make the tart cases and the cheesecake mixture the night before and store them separately to assemble the next day. Keep the cheesecake filling refrigerated and the tart cases in an airtight container.

Slice the fruit and place it on to each tart right before serving.

DRINKS

❀ MERTASTIC MILKSHAKE ❀

This indulgent sweet masterpiece is one seriously special treat. Let your creativity run wild and serve this chilled drink with a generous dollop of whipped cream, some sprinkles and a chocolate mermaid tail.

Serves: 2 ❀ Time: 30 minutes ❀ Difficulty rating: ★

INGREDIENTS

* 50g white chocolate
* Pink gel food colouring
* 50g dark chocolate
* 6 scoops vanilla ice cream
* 10 strawberries, hulled and chopped
* 200ml semi-skimmed milk
* Whipped cream from a can
* Hundreds and thousands

EXTRA EQUIPMENT

You will need two mermaid tail moulds, a piping bag, a small round-tip nozzle, a blender and two large wine glasses.

METHOD

Melt the white chocolate in a bowl set over a pan of simmering water or in a microwave. Once melted, add a few drops of the pink gel food colouring to the chocolate and mix until it is completely pink. Fill the mermaid moulds with the pink chocolate and leave in the freezer to set for 5 minutes.

Now melt the dark chocolate in a bowl set over a pan of simmering water or in a microwave. Transfer half the dark chocolate into a piping bag fixed with a small round-tip nozzle.

Prepare each glass by piping the chocolate in straight lines, from the bottom to the top of the inside of the glass, then dip the rim in the rest of the melted chocolate and coat it with hundreds and thousands before the chocolate hardens.

Put the vanilla ice cream, strawberries and milk in a blender and blitz until smooth.

Pour into your prepared glass and top with a generous dose of squirty cream and, yes, you guessed it, more sprinkles.

Finally, top with the chocolate mermaid tails.

🐚 SEA BREEZE SLUSHIE 🐚

Feel as cool as a cucumber with this delicately flavoured and super-healthy smoothie.

Serves: 2 🐚 Time: 15 minutes 🐚 Difficulty rating: ⭐

INGREDIENTS

* 1 cucumber, peeled and cubed
* Juice of 1 lime
* 6–8 mint leaves
* Ice to fill 2 glasses
* Sparkling water to fill 2 glasses
* Agave syrup (optional)

EXTRA EQUIPMENT

You will need a blender and two large wine glasses (copa glasses are my preferred choice for this drink).

METHOD

Add the cucumber, lime juice, mint, ice and sparkling water to a blender.

Blitz for 1 minute until there are no large lumps of ice remaining, then pour the drink into the two glasses.

Serve with a slice of cucumber and sprig of mint and drink immediately.

This is a deliciously refreshing drink, but if you wish to add a touch of sweetener, add a squeeze of agave syrup to the mixture during the blending stage.

⚜ LEMONADE FLOAT ⚜

When a dip in the ocean isn't possible, this thirst-quenching classic is the best way to cool down on a hot day.

Serves: 6 ⚜ Time: 15 minutes ⚜ Difficulty rating: ★

INGREDIENTS

* ★ 100g granulated sugar
* ★ 1 litre water
* ★ 100ml lemon juice (about 4 lemons)
* ★ A few handfuls of ice
* ★ 1 tub vanilla ice cream

EXTRA EQUIPMENT

You will need a large jug and an ice-cream scoop.

METHOD

In a small pan, combine the sugar and 100ml water and bring to a simmer until the sugar dissolves. Remove from the heat and allow to cool to room temperature.

In a large jug, stir together the remaining water with the cooled simple syrup and lemon juice.

Pour into ice-filled glasses and top with scoops of vanilla ice cream.

Serve with a stripy straw and enjoy immediately.

❧ SEALICIOUS CHIA SEED SMOOTHIE ❧

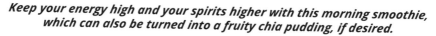

Keep your energy high and your spirits higher with this morning smoothie,
which can also be turned into a fruity chia pudding, if desired.

Serves: 2 ❧ Time: 30 minutes, plus 4 hours 10 minutes cooling time ❧
Difficulty rating: ★

INGREDIENTS

* ★ 3 tbsp chia seeds
* ★ 450ml plant milk (almond, coconut, soya or oat)
* ★ 1 tbsp honey
* ★ 200g frozen blueberries
* ★ 300g strawberries
* ★ 2 bananas

EXTRA EQUIPMENT

You will need a blender and two 250ml glasses.

METHOD

For the chia pudding:

Pour the chia seeds, 250ml plant milk of choice and honey into a jug or bowl and mix well. Let it settle for 2–3 minutes then mix again until there are no lumps.

Cover the jug or bowl and leave in the fridge for 4 hours (or overnight if possible).

For the blueberry layer:

Before taking the chia pudding out of the fridge, prepare your blueberry layer by adding 200g of frozen blueberries and 100ml of plant milk to a blender. Blitz until smooth then spoon out into your serving glass. Pop into the freezer for 10 minutes.

For the chia pudding layer:

When the blueberry layer has chilled for 10 minutes, remove from the freezer and pour the chia layer on top of the blueberry layer, dividing the mixture equally between the two serving glasses. Slice six strawberries thinly and carefully position them against the glass on top of the chia layer. Put the glasses in the fridge.

For the strawberry/banana layer:

Put the banana and remaining strawberries into a blender with 100ml of plant milk and blitz until smooth.

Divide the mixture equally between the two glasses and serve immediately.

(Note: turn this into a chia pudding by doubling the amount of chia mixture and splitting half the thickened chia pudding equally between the blueberry and strawberry layer. Layer the flavours as usual but leave them in the fridge to set for an extra 30 minutes before serving.)

MY RECIPE NOTES

INDEX

bars
    coconut **71**
    crispy marshmallow **83**
biscuits
    chocolate cookies **51**
    ginger **55**
    jam **46**
    mermaid tail **93**
    oyster **52**
bites
    energy balls **63**
    mermaid rocks **73**
    pretzel **58**
    rocky road **91**
bread
    toast **103**
brownies **64**
cake pops **85**
cakes
    basic sponge **18, 20, 22, 32, 35, 38**
    mirror glaze **29**
    two tier **41**
cheesecake **113**

churros **88**
cupcakes
    coconut **20**
    lemon **18**
    lime **22**
    raspberry **16**
decorations
    coconut **12, 20, 63, 71, 107, 120**
    edible eyes **11, 20, 55, 68, 109**
    edible sand **35–37, 41–44, 55–56**
    glitter **11, 18, 22, 38, 71, 73, 83, 85**
    ice-cream cones **41–44**
    Mermaid Kisses **29–31, 32–33, 60–61**
    pearl sprinkles **22, 67, 73, 83**
    sugar-coated chocolate drops **68**
doughnuts **68**
drinks
    float **131**
    milkshake **127**
    slushie **129**
    smoothie **133**
eclairs **78**
fruit kebabs **81**

fudge 67

ice lollies 119

icing

    buttercream 12–13, 16–17, 18–19, 20–21, 22–23, 25–26, 29–30, 32–33, 35–37, 38–39, 41–43, 52–53, 76–77, 78–79

    fondant 41, 46, 52, 113

    royal 48, 93

jelly 99, 113

macarons 76

madeleines 97

mousse 117

pancakes 104

shortbread 48

smoothies

    chia seed and berries 133

    cucumber and mint 129

    tropical fruit 107

Swiss roll 120

tart 123

waffles 109

If you're interested in finding out more
about our books, find us on Facebook
at SUMMERSDALE PUBLISHERS and
follow us on Twitter at @SUMMERSDALE.

WWW.SUMMERSDALE.COM